CHIANG MAI PROVINCE

Books LLC®, Reference Series, Memphis, USA, 2011. ISBN: 9781156090060. www.booksllc.net. Copyright: http://creativecommons.org/licenses/by-sa/3.0/deed.en

Table of Contents

Amphoe of Chiang Mai
Chai Prakan District 3
Chiang Dao District 3
Chom Thong District, Chiang Mai Province 3
Doi Lo District 4
Doi Saket District 4
Doi Tao District 4
Fang District 5
Galyani Vadhana District 5
Hang Dong District 6
Hot District 6
Mae Ai District 6
Mae Chaem District 7
Mae On District 7
Mae Rim District 7
Mae Taeng District 8
Mae Wang District 8
Mueang Chiang Mai District 8
Omkoi District 9
Phrao District 9
Samoeng District 9
San Kamphaeng District 10
San Pa Tong District 10
San Sai District 10
Saraphi District 10
Wiang Haeng District 11

Buddhist temples in Chiang Mai Province
Wat Aranyawiwake 11
Wat Doi Mae Pang 11

Chiang Mai
Baan Haw Mosque 11
Badminton at the 1995 Southeast Asian Games 12
Bhubing Palace 12
Chiang Mai 12
Chiang Mai Creative City 18
Chiang Mai Initiative 20
Chiang Mai International Airport 21
Chiang Mai LRT 21
Chiang Mai Metropolitan Area 22
Chiang Mai Night Bazaar 22
Chiang Mai Night Safari 22

Chiang Mai Rajabhat University 23
Chiang Mai University 23
Chiang Mai Zoo 25
Chiang Mai Zoo Monorail 25
Chiangmai F.C. 25
Dara Academy 25
Darunaman Mosque 26
Dokmai Garden 27
Inthakin 27
Maejo University 27
Montfort College 28
North Chiang Mai University 28
Payap University 28
Rajamangala University of Technology Lanna 29
Roman Catholic Diocese of Chiang Mai 30
Royal Flora Ratchaphruek 31
Wiang Kum Kam 32

Chiang Mai Province
Chiang Mai Province 32
Doi Inthanon 37
Doi Suthep 38
Mae Taeng River 38
Ping River 38
Queen Sirikit Botanic Garden 39

Tambon of Chiang Mai Province
Ban Aen 39
Ban Chan, Galyani Vadhana 39
Ban Chang, Mae Taeng 39
Ban Kat, Mae Wang 39
Ban Klang, San Pa Tong 39
Ban Luang, Chom Thong 39
Ban Luang, Mae Ai 40
Ban Mae 40
Ban Pae 40
Ban Pao, Mae Taeng 40
Ban Pong, Hang Dong 40
Ban Pong, Phrao 40
Ban Sahakon 40
Ban Tan, Hot 40
Ban Thap 41
Ban Waen 41
Bo Kaeo, Samoeng 41

Bo Luang 41
Bo Sali 41
Bong Tan 41
Buak Khang 41
Chae Chang 41
Chaem Luang 42
Chai Sathan 42
Chang Khlan 42
Chang Khoeng 42
Chang Moi 42
Chang Phueak, Mueang Chiang Mai 42
Chiang Dao 42
Cho Lae 42
Choeng Doi 43
Chom Phu 43
Doi Kaeo 43
Doi Lo 43
Doi Tao 43
Don Kaeo, Mae Rim 43
Don Kaeo, Saraphi 43
Don Pao 43
Fa Ham 44
Haiya 44
Han Kaeo 44
Hang Dong, Hang Dong 44
Hang Dong, Hot 44
Hot, Hot 44
Huai Kaeo, Mae On 44
Huai Sai, Mae Rim 44
Huai Sai, San Kamphaeng 45
Inthakhin 45
Khilek, Mae Rim 45
Khilek, Mae Taeng 45
Khua Mung 45
Khuang Pao 45
Khuean Phak 45
Khun Khong 46
Kong Khaek 46
Kuet Chang 46
Long Khot 46
Luang Nuea 46
Mae Ai 46
Mae Daet 46
Mae Faek 46
Mae Faek Mai 47
Mae Hia 47

Mae Ho Phra 47	Nong Hoi 53	San Phi Suea 59
Mae Hoi Ngoen 47	Nong Kaeo, Hang Dong 53	San Phranet 59
Mae Ka 47	Nong Khwai 53	San Pong 59
Mae Ka, Fang 47	Nong Pa Khrang 53	San Pu Loei 59
Mae Khue 47	Nong Phueng 54	San Sai, Fang 60
Mae Na 47	Nong Tong 54	San Sai, Phrao 60
Mae Na Chon 48	Nong Yaeng 54	San Sai, Saraphi 60
Mae Na Wang 48	Omkoi 54	San Sai Luang 60
Mae Ngon 48	On Klang 54	San Sai Noi 60
Mae Pang 48	On Nuea 54	San Ton Mue 60
Mae Pong 48	On Tai 54	Santi Suk 60
Mae Pu Kha 48	Pa Bong 54	Saraphi 60
Mae Raem 49	Pa Daet, Mueang Chiang Mai .. 55	Si Dong Yen 61
Mae Sa 49	Pa Lan 55	Si Phum 61
Mae Sao 49	Pa Miang 55	Song Khwae 61
Mae Sap 49	Pa Nai 55	Sop Khong 61
Mae Soi 49	Pa Pae 55	Sop Mae Kha 61
Mae Suek 49	Pa Phai 55	Sop Poeng 61
Mae Sun 49	Pa Pong, Doi Saket 55	Sop Tia 61
Mae Taeng 50	Pa Tan, Chiang Mai 56	Suthep 61
Mae Tha 50	Pa Tum 56	Talat Khwan 62
Mae Thalop 50	Pang Hin Fon 56	Talat Yai 62
Mae Tuen 50	Phra Sing 56	Tha Duea 62
Mae Waen 50	Piang Luang 56	Tha Kwang 62
Mae Win 50	Ping Khong 56	Tha Nuea 62
Makham Luang 50	Pong Nam Ron, Fang 56	Tha Pha, Mae Chaem 62
Makhun Wan 50	Pong Tam 56	Tha Sala, Mueang Chiang Mai. 62
Malika, Thailand 51	Pong Thung 57	Tha Ton 62
Mon Chong 51	Pong Yaeng 57	Tha Wang Phrao 63
Mon Pin 51	Rim Nuea 57	Tha Wang Tan 63
Mueang Haeng 51	Rim Tai 57	Thep Sadet 63
Mueang Kaeo 51	Rong Wua Daeng 57	Thung Khao Phuang 63
Mueang Kai 51	Sa-nga Ban 57	Thung Luang, Phrao 63
Mueang Khong 51	Saen Hai 57	Thung Pi 63
Mueang Len 51	Sai Mun, San Kamphaeng ... 57	Thung Ruang Thong, Mae Wang. 64
Mueang Na 52	Saluang, Mae Rim 58	Thung Satok 64
Mueang Ngai 52	Samoeng Nuea 58	Thung Tom 64
Muet Ka 52	Samoeng Tai 58	Ton Pao 64
Na Kho Ruea 52	Samran Rat 58	Wat Ket 64
Na Kian 52	San Kamphaeng 58	Wiang, Fang 64
Nam Bo Luang 52	San Klang, San Kamphaeng . 58	Wiang, Phrao 64
Nam Phrae, Hang Dong 52	San Klang, San Pa Tong ... 58	Yang Khram 64
Nam Phrae, Phrao 52	San Maha Phon 58	Yang Moen 65
Nong Bua, Chai Prakan 53	San Na Meng 59	Yang Noeng 65
Nong Chom 53	San Pa Pao 59	Yang Piang 65
Nong Faek 53	San Pa Yang 59	Yu Wa 65
Nong Han, San Sai 53	San Phak Wan 59	

Introduction

Purchase of this book entitles you to a free trial membership in the publisher's book club at www.booksllc.net. (Time limited offer.) Simply enter the barcode number from the back cover onto the membership form. The book club entitles you to select from hundreds of thousands of books at no additional charge. You can also download a digital copy of this and related books to read on the go.

Simply enter the title or subject onto the search form to find them.

Each chapter in this book ends with a URL to a hyperlinked online version. Type the URL exactly as it appears. If

you change the URL's capitalization it won't work. Use the online version to access related pages, websites, footnotes, tables, color photos, updates. Click the version history tab to see the chapter's contributors. Click the edit link to suggest changes.

A large and diverse editor base collaboratively wrote the book, not a single author. After a long process of discussion and debate, the chapters gradually took on a neutral point of view reached through consensus. Additional editors expanded and contributed to chapters striving to achieve balance and comprehensive coverage. This reduced the regional or cultural bias found in many other books and provided access and breadth on subject matter otherwise little documented.

Chai Prakan District

Chai Prakan (Thai: ไชยปราการ) is a district (*amphoe*) in the northern part of Chiang Mai Province in northern Thailand.

Geography
Neighboring districts are (from the south clockwise) Phrao, Chiang Dao, Fang of Chiang Mai Province and Mae Suai of Chiang Rai Province.

History
The minor district (*King Amphoe*) Chai Prakan was created on January 1, 1988, when four *tambon* were split off from Fang district. It was upgraded to a full district on July 4, 1994.

Administration
The district is subdivided into 4 subdistricts (*tambon*), which are further subdivided into 43 villages (*muban*). Chai Prakan itself is a township (*thesaban tambon*) which covers parts of the *tambon* Pong Tam, Si Dong Yen and Nong Bua. There are further 3 Tambon administrative organizations (TAO).
Source (edited): "http://en.wikipedia.org/wiki/Chai_Prakan_District"

Chiang Dao District

Chiang Dao (Thai: เชียงดาว) is a district (*amphoe*) of Chiang Mai Province in northern Thailand. It is nicknamed "Little Tuscany" and there are actually a few local wines produced in the area.

Geography
Neighboring districts are (from the northeast clockwise) Fang, Chai Prakan, Phrao, Mae Taeng of Chiang Mai Province, Pai of Mae Hong Son Province, and Wiang Haeng of Chiang Mai again. To the north is the Shan State of Myanmar.

An interesting fact, Chiang Dao is the only province in Thailand that has all twelve hill tribes in residence.

The Pha Daeng National Park is located in the district.

History
Chiang Dao was a smaller city state (*Mueang*) in the northern Thai Lan Na kingdom. As part of the *thesaphiban* administrative reforms at the end of the 19th century it was made a district within Chiang Mai province.

Originally a minor district (*King Amphoe*), it was upgraded to a full district in 1908.

Administration
The district is subdivided into 7 subdistricts (*tambon*), which are further subdivided into 83 villages (*muban*). Both Chiang Dao and Mueang Ngai are subdistrict municipalities (*thesaban tambon*), which cover parts of the same-named *tambon*. The subdistrict municipality Phra That Pu Kam (พระธาตุปู่ก่ำ) covers the remaining parts of the subdistrict Mueang Ngai. Mueang Na, Ping Khong and Thung Khao Phuang are further subdistrict municipalities which cover the whole same-named subdistrict. There are further 3 Tambon administrative organizations (TAO) - Mae Na and Mueang Khong covering the whole same-named subdistrict, and Chiang Dao the non-municipal parts of the subdistrict.
Source (edited): "http://en.wikipedia.org/wiki/Chiang_Dao_District"

Chom Thong District, Chiang Mai Province

Chom Thong (Thai: จอมทอง) is a district (*amphoe*) in the southern part of Chiang Mai Province in northern Thailand.

History
According to the legend of *Wat Phra That Si Chom Thong Worawihan*, the location of the temple is on a small hill which looks similar to a termite hill (*Chom Pluak* in Thai). The hill is covered by *Thong Kwao* or Bastard teak (*Butea monosperma*) and *Thong Lang* or Coral trees (*Erythrina variegata*) forest. Thus the people called the hill Chom Thong.

After Lord Buddha entered parinirvana, King Asoka the Great visited the hill to place Buddha's relics there. The temple was built on the hill and named Wat Phra That Chom Thong in 1451. Later the temple was upgraded to be Royal temple and at the same time renamed to Wat Phra That Si Chom Thong Worawihan.

The government created a district in the area in 1900 and named the new dis-

trict Chom Thong following the legend. The district office was originally located in Ban Tha Sala, Tambon Khuang Pao. In 1933 the office was moved to the southwest of Wat Phra That Chom Thong.

Geography

Neighboring districts are (from the south clockwise) Hot, Mae Chaem, Mae Wang, Doi Lo of Chiang Mai Province, Wiang Nong Long and Ban Hong of Lamphun Province.

The important river is the Ping River.

The Doi Inthanon National Park is located in the district.

Administration

The district is subdivided into 6 subdistricts (*tambon*), which are further subdivided into 96 villages (*muban*). Chom Thong is a township (*thesaban tambon*), which covers parts of *tambon* Ban Luang, Khuan Pao and Doi Kaeo. There are further 6 Tambon administrative organizations (TAO).

Missing numbers are *tambon* which now form Doi Lo district.

Source (edited): "http://en.wikipedia.org/wiki/Chom_Thong_District,_Chiang_Mai_Province"

Doi Lo District

Doi Lo (Thai: ดอยหล่อ) is a district (*amphoe*) of Chiang Mai Province in northern Thailand.

Geography

Neighboring districts are (from the southwest clockwise) Chom Thong, Mae Wang, San Pa Tong of Chiang Mai Province, Pa Sang and Wiang Nong Long of Lamphun Province.

History

The minor district (*King Amphoe*) was established on April 1, 1995, when four *tambon* were split off from Chom Thong.

Following a decision of the Thai government on May 15, 2007, all of the 81 minor districts were to be upgraded to full districts. With the publishing in the Royal Gazette on August 24 the upgrade became official .

Administration

The district is subdivided into 4 subdistricts (*tambon*), which are further subdivided into 54 villages (*muban*). There are no municipal (*thesaban*) areas, and 4 Tambon administrative organizations (TAO).

Source (edited): "http://en.wikipedia.org/wiki/Doi_Lo_District"

Doi Saket District

Doi Saket (Thai: ดอยสะเก็ด) is a district (*amphoe*) in the eastern part of Chiang Mai Province in northern Thailand.

History

The district was established in 1902.

Geography

Neighboring districts are (from the south clockwise) Mae On, San Kamphaeng, San Sai, Mae Taeng, Phrao of Chiang Mai Province, Wiang Pa Pao of Chiang Rai Province and Mueang Pan of Lampang Province.

Life Style

The district is predominantly a rural farming area, containing a mixture of rice fields on the valley floor to orchard and other farming on the hillsides. The village proper is located a 30 minute drive east from Tha Pae Gate in Chiang Mai. It has some service providers for businesses in the neighboring city, such as a commercial laundry for Chiang Mai's hotels and a concrete production facility. However, the town's economic focus is still agricultural, and the city boasts a large produce market. The village is most famous with Thai tourists for its beautiful, modern-style wall murals inside of Wat Doi Saket.

Administration

The district is subdivided into 14 subdistricts (*tambon*), which are further subdivided into 110 villages (*muban*). Doi Saket is a township (*thesaban tambon*), which covers parts of *tambon* Choeng Doi and Luang Nuea. There are further 13 Tambon administrative organizations (TAO).

Source (edited): "http://en.wikipedia.org/wiki/Doi_Saket_District"

Doi Tao District

Doi Tao (Thai: ดอยเต่า) is a district (*amphoe*) in the southern part of Chiang Mai Province in northern Thailand.

Geography

Neighboring districts are (from the west clockwise) Om Koi, Hot of Chiang Mai Province, Li of Lamphun Province and Sam Ngao of Tak Province.

History

The minor district (*King Amphoe*) was established on October 16, 1972 by splitting off the four *tambon* Tha Duea, Doi Tao, Muet Ka and Ban Aen from Hot district. It was upgraded to a full district on March 25, 1979.

Administration

The district is subdivided into 6 subdistricts (*tambon*), which are further sub-

divided into 42 villages (*muban*). Tha Duea is a township (*thesaban tambon*) which covers parts of the *tambon* Tha Duea and Mueat Ka. There are further 5 Tambon administrative organizations (TAO).

Source (edited): "http://en.wikipedia.org/wiki/Doi_Tao_District"

Fang District

Fang (Thai: ฝาง Northern Thai: ????) is a district (*amphoe*) in the northern part of Chiang Mai Province, northern Thailand.

History

According to the Yonok chronicle, *Mueang* Fang was built in 641 by King Lawa Changkarat. Later King Mengrai the Great reigned Fang before building Wiang Kumkam and Chiang Mai of Lanna Kingdom for one year around 1268. It seems that Mengrai used Mueang Fang for the base to invade Hariphunchai.

In 1910 the *Mueang* Fang was made a subordinate of Chiang Rai, then named Mueang Fang district. In 1925 it was reassigned to Chiang Mai. 1938 it the word *Mueang* was cut off from the name, which was then reserved for the capital districts on the provinces.

Etymology

The landscape of Mueang Fang looked like the seed of a Fang tree (*Caesalpinia sappan*). Thus the town was named after the tree.

Geography

Neighboring districts are (from the northeast clockwise) Mae Ai of Chiang Mai Province, Mae Suai of Chiang Rai Province, Chai Prakan of Chiang Mai Province again and Shan State of Myanmar.

The Doi Phahompok National Park is located in Fang district.

Administration

The district is subdivided into 8 subdistricts (*tambon*), which are further subdivided into 128 villages (*muban*). There are two townships (*thesaban tambon*) - Wiang Phrao covers parts of *tambon* Wiang, and Ban Mae Kha parts of *tambon* Mae Kha. There are further 8 Tambon administrative organizations (TAO).

Missing numbers belong to *tambon* which now form Chai Prakan.

Source (edited): "http://en.wikipedia.org/wiki/Fang_District"

Galyani Vadhana District

Galyani Vadhana (Thai: กัลยาณิวัฒนา; RTGS: Kanlayaniwatthana) is a district (*amphoe*) of Chiang Mai Province in northern Thailand. It is named after the Princess Galyani Vadhana. It was founded on December 26, 2009, making it the 878th and latest district of Thailand.

History

The project of creating a new district in the area dates back to 1993. On May 17 1993 the Tambon council of Ban Chan subdistrict proposed the creation of the minor district out of three subdistricts of Mae Chaem district. In the following years its creation was prepared, however with the onset of the Asian financial crisis in 1997 all pending new districts were canceled by the government in order to avoid additional costs.

Around 2005 the project came on the agenda again and proposals and studies were done by Chiang Mai province and the Department of Provincial Administration. December 2 2008 the cabinet approved in principle the creation of the new district in honor of Princess Galyani Vadhana as proposed by the Ministry of Interior.

On July 7 2009 King Bhumibol Adulyadej officially bestowed the name Galyani Vadhana on the new district, which was previously referred to by the name Wat Chan (วัดจันทร์). In the cabinet meeting on October 13 the Ministry of Interior was authorized to set up the new district.

Due to the fact that in has a royal project in Ban Chan, the new district did not need to be a sub-district (*King Amphoe*) at first and could be created as a full district directly. The district office is under construction in Village 2 of Chaem Luang subdistrict. Until its completion, the rooms of the subdistrict council Ban Chan will be used as a temporary district office.

The Abhisit Government completed drawing up a draft Royal Decree Establishing Amphoe Galyani Vadhana on October 13, 2009 and King Bhumibol Adulyadej signed it on December 18 of the same year. The **"Royal Decree Establishing Amphoe Galyani Vadhana, Changwat Chiang Mai, BE 2552 (2009)"** was published in the Government Gazette volume 126/part 97 A/page 7/dated December 25, 2009 and came into force as of the following day.

Geography

Neighboring districts are (from the east clockwise) Samoeng and Mae Chaem of Chiang Mai Province, and Mueang Mae Hong Son and Pai of Mae Hong Son Province.

The district is located within the mountains of the Doi Inthanon range, with the settlements mostly in the valleys.

Administration

The district is subdivided into three subdistricts (*Tambon*), which are further subdivided into 23 villages (*muban*). Each of the subdistricts is administrated by a Tambon administrative organization (TAO).

Source (edited): "http://en.wikipedia.

Hang Dong District

Hang Dong (Thai: หางดง) is a district (*amphoe*) of Chiang Mai Province in northern Thailand.

Geography
Neighboring districts are (from the southwest clockwise) San Pa Tong, Mae Wang, Samoeng, Mae Rim, Mueang Chiang Mai, Saraphi of Chiang Mai Province and Mueang Lamphun of Lamphun Province.

To reach Baan Tawaii. (famous Handicraft center) you turn left just after Hang Dong market if you are driving from Chiang Mai. Hang Dong has a 9 hole golf course located on the canal road.

Administration
The district is subdivided into 11 sub-districts (*tambon*), which are further subdivided into 113 villages (*muban*). Nong Thong Phattana is a township (*thesaban tambon*), which covers parts of *tambon* Nong Thong. There are further 10 Tambon administrative organizations (TAO).

Gallery

The beautiful Wat Ton Kwaen from 1858 CE, only 8 km south-west of Chiang Mai's city walls, in Hang Dong

Detail of the wihan building of Wat Ton Kwaen showing the wood carving
Source (edited): "http://en.wikipedia.org/wiki/Hang_Dong_District"

Hot District

Hot (Thai: ฮอด) is a district (*amphoe*) in the southern part of Chiang Mai Province in northern Thailand.

Geography
Neighboring districts are (from the north clockwise) Mae Chaem, Chom Thong of Chiang Mai Province, Ban Hong, Li of Lamphun Province, Doi Tao, Omkoi of Chiang Mai Province again, Sop Moei and Mae Sariang of Mae Hong Son Province.

History
In 1905 the district Muet Ka was abolished and split into the district Mueang Hot and the minor district Mueang Hot. In 1917 the district was renamed to Hot.

Administration
The district is subdivided into 6 subdistricts (*tambon*), which are further subdivided into 60 villages (*muban*). There are two subdistrict municipalities (*thesaban tambon*) - Tha Kham and Hang Dong, both covering parts of *tambon* Hang Don. There are further 6 Tambon administrative organizations (TAO).
Source (edited): "http://en.wikipedia.org/wiki/Hot_District"

Mae Ai District

Mae Ai (Thai: แม่อาย) is the northernmost district (*amphoe*) of Chiang Mai Province, northern Thailand.

History
The minor district (*King Amphoe*) Mae Ai was created on August 15, 1967, when the three *tambon* Mae Ai, Mae Sao and Mae Na Wang were separated from Fang district. It was official upgraded to a full district on June 28, 1973.

Geography

The Kok River in Amphoe Mae Ai

Neighboring districts are (from the southwest clockwise) Fang of Chiang Mai Province, Shan State of Myanmar, Mae Fa Luang, Mueang Chiang Rai and Mae Suai of Chiang Rai Province.

The important rivers are the Kok and Fang river.

Administration
The district is subdivided into 7 communes (*tambon*), which are further subdivided into 110 villages (*muban*). Mai Ai is also a township (*thesaban tambon*), which covers parts of the *tambon* Mae Ai and Malika. There are further 6 Tambon administrative organizations

(TAO).

Source (edited): "http://en.wikipedia.org/wiki/Mae_Ai_District"

Mae Chaem District

Mae Chaem (Thai: แม่แจ่ม) is a district (*amphoe*) of Chiang Mai Province in northern Thailand.

History

Rice paddies and recently cleared forest land along road 1263 in Mae Chaem district during the 2010 dry season

The district Mueang Chaem was created in 1908, consisting of the *tambon* Mae Thap, Tha Pha, Chang Khoeng and Mae Suek split off from Chom Thong. In 1917 it was renamed to Chang Khoeng, as the district office was located in that *tambon*. In 1938 it was reduced to a minor district (*King Amphoe*) and was a subordinate of Chom Thong district. 1939 it was renamed to Mae Chaem. In 1956 it was upgraded to a full district.

In 2009 the northern part of the district was split off to form the new district Galyani Vadhana.

Geography

Neighboring districts are (from the north clockwise) Galyani Vadhana, Samoeng, Mae Wang, Chom Thong and Hot of Chiang Mai Province, and Mae Sariang, Mae La Noi, Khun Yuam, Mueang Mae Hong Son and Pai of Mae Hong Son Province.

Thailand's highest mountain, 2.565 meter (8,415 ft) high Doi Inthanon, is located in Mae Chaem district.

Administration

The river going through the town of Mae Chaem

The district is subdivided into 7 subdistricts (*tambon*), which are further subdivided into 85 villages (*muban*). Mae Chaem also has subdistrict municipality (*thesaban tambon*) status and covers parts of *tambon* Chang Khoeng. There are further 7 Tambon administrative organizations (TAO).

Missing numbers belong to the subdistricts which formed Galyani Vadhana district in 2009.

Source (edited): "http://en.wikipedia.org/wiki/Mae_Chaem_District"

Mae On District

Mae On is a district (*amphoe*) of Chiang Mai Province in the north of Thailand.

Geography

The district is located about 40 km east of the city Chiang Mai. Neighboring districts are (from the west clockwise) San Kamphaeng and Doi Saket (Chiang Mai Province), Mueang Pan and Mueang Lampang of Lampang Province, Ban Thi, Mueang Lamphun and Mae Tha of Lamphun Province.

The Mai Ta Khai National Park protecting the source of the Ping River is located in this district.

Mae On is a popular destination for rock climbers who wish to climb the limestone cliffs of Crazy Horse Buttress. Rock climbing at Crazy Horse has greatly expanded since 2000 due to the work of Joshua Morris and Khaetthaleeya Uppakham while writing their book, *A Guide to Rock Climbing in Northern Thailand*. Other tourist attractions of the town include natural hot springs and the Mae On cave system.

History

The minor district (*King Amphoe*) was created on April 30, 1994, when six *tambon* were split off from San Kamphaeng district.

Following a decision of the Thai government on May 15, 2007, all of the 81 minor districts were to be upgraded to full districts. With the publishing in the Royal Gazette on August 24 the upgrade became official.

Administration

The district is subdivided into 6 subdistricts (*tambon*), which are further subdivided into 49 villages (*muban*). There are no municipal (*thesaban*) areas. Each of the *tambon* is led by a tambon administrative organization (TAO).

Source (edited): "http://en.wikipedia.org/wiki/Mae_On_District"

Mae Rim District

Mae Rim (Thai: แม่ริม) is a district (*amphoe*) in the central part of Chiang Mai Province in northern Thailand.

History

Formerly the district was called *Khwaeng* Mae Rim. *Khwaeng* Mae Rim coverted to full district (*amphoe*) in 1914.

Geography

Neighboring districts are (from the north clockwise) Mae Taeng, San Sai, Mueang Chiang Mai, Hang Dong and Samoeng of Chiang Mai Province.

Administration

The district is subdivided into 11 subdistricts (*tambon*), which are further subdivided into 91 villages (*muban*). Mae Rim is a township (*thesaban tambon*), which covers parts of *tambon* Rim Tai and Mae Sa. There are further 10 Tambon administrative organizations (TAO).

Source (edited): "http://en.wikipedia.org/wiki/Mae_Rim_District"

Mae Taeng District

Mae Taeng (Thai: แม่แตง) is a district (*amphoe*) in the northern part of Chiang Mai Province in northern Thailand.

Geography

Neighboring districts are (from the north clockwise) Chiang Dao, Phrao, Doi Saket, San Sai, Mae Rim, Samoeng of Chiang Mai Province and Pai of Mae Hong Son Province.

History

In 1892, *Khwaeng* Mueang Kuet (เมืองกื้ด) was created, and renamed in 1894 to *Khwaeng* Mueang Kaen (เมืองแกน). In 1907 it was upgraded to a district (*amphoe*) named San Maha Phon (สันมหาพน), and renamed Mae Tang in 1939.

Administration

The district is subdivided into 13 subdistricts (*tambon*), which are further subdivided into 128 villages (*muban*). There are two townships (*thesaban tambon*) - San Maha Phon covers parts of *tambon* San Maha Phon and Khilek; Mueang Kaen Phatthana covers the whole *tambon* Cho Lae and parts of Intha Khin. There are further 11 Tambon administrative organizations (TAO).

Source (edited): "http://en.wikipedia.org/wiki/Mae_Taeng_District"

Mae Wang District

Mae Wang (Thai: แม่วาง) is a district (*amphoe*) in the central part of Chiang Mai Province in northern Thailand.

Geography

Neighboring districts are (from the south clockwise) Doi Lo, Chom Thong, Mae Chaem, Samoeng, Hang Dong and San Pa Tong of Chiang Mai Province.

History

The minor district (*King Amphoe*) was established on April 1, 1990, when the four *tambon* Ban Kat, Thung Pi, Thung Ruang Thong and Mae Win were split off from San Pa Tong district. On September 7, 1995 it was upgraded to a full district.

Administration

The district is subdivided into 5 subdistricts (*tambon*), which are further subdivided into 62 villages (*muban*). Ban Kat is a township (*thesaban tambon*) which covers parts of the *tambon* Ban Kat and Don Pao. There are further 5 Tambon administrative organizations (TAO).

Source (edited): "http://en.wikipedia.org/wiki/Mae_Wang_District"

Mueang Chiang Mai District

Mueang Chiang Mai (Thai: เมืองเชียงใหม่) is the capital district (*amphoe mueang*) of Chiang Mai Province in northern Thailand. The district contains the city of Chiang Mai.

History

The area of *Mueang* Chiang Mai district was the central part of the Lanna Kingdom, named Nopphaburi Si Nakhon Phing Chiang Mai. King Mengrai the Great was the first king of the Mengrai dynasty, who established the city.

The government created Mueang Chiang Mai district in 1899. The first district office was opened in 1929, on the west side of the old city hall of Chiang Mai. A new district office was opened in August 1989.

Geography

Neighboring districts are (from the north clockwise) Mae Rim, San Sai, San Kamphaeng, Saraphi and Hang Dong.

The main river through the district is the Ping River.

Administration

The district is subdivided into 16 subdistricts (*tambon*), which are further subdivided into 77 villages (*muban*). The city (*thesaban nakhon*) Chiang Mai covers the *tambon* Si Phum, Phra Sing, Haiya, Chiang Moi, Chang Khlan, Wat Ket and Pa Tan, and parts of the *tambon* Chang Phueak, Suthep, Pa Daet, Nong Hoi, Tha Sala, Nong Pa Khrang and Fa Ham. There are further 3 townships (*thesaban tambon*) - Chang Phueak covers parts of the *tambon* Chang Phueak, and Mae Hia and Tha Sala the whole same-named *tambon*. There are further 6 Tambon administrative organizations (TAO).

Source (edited): "http://en.wikipedia.org/wiki/Mueang_Chiang_Mai_District"

Omkoi District

Omkoi (Thai: อมก๋อย) is the southwesternmost district (*amphoe*) of Chiang Mai Province in northern Thailand.

Geography
Neighboring districts are (from the north clockwise) Hot, Doi Tao of Chiang Mai Province, Sam Ngao, Mae Ramat Tha Song Yang of Tak Province and Sop Moei of Mae Hong Son Province.

History
The minor district (*King Amphoe*) was established on April 19 1929 as a subordinate of Hot district, consisting of the three subdistricts Omkoi, Yang Piang and Mae Tun. It was upgraded to a full district on July 23 1958.

Administration
The district is subdivided into 6 subdistricts (*tambon*), which are further subdivided into 95 villages (*muban*). Omkoi is a subdistrict municipality (*thesaban tambon*) which covers parts of the *tambon* Omkoi. There are further 6 Tambon administrative organizations (TAO).

Gallery

Pine forests along road 108 near the intersection to Omkoi

Road 1099 eventually ends in the jungle at Mae Thun Noi, Amphoe Omkoi
Source (edited): "http://en.wikipedia.org/wiki/Omkoi_District"

Phrao District

Phrao (Thai: พร้าว) is a district (*amphoe*) in the northeastern part of Chiang Mai Province in northern Thailand.

History
The name *Phrao* was given to this city around 1281 by King Mangrai of Lan Na kingdom who has been on the way to invade Hariphunchai Kingdom. After this, Mangrai sent his third son, Khrua to rule Phrao. Hereafter, Phrao become one of important city of Lan Na kingdom.

King Tilokarat, who is considered a god-king of Lan Na, once have ruled this city before becoming a king.

Geography
Neighboring districts are (from the south clockwise) Doi Saket, Mae Taeng, Chiang Dao, Chai Prakan of Chiang Mai Province, Mae Suai and Wiang Pa Pao of Chiang Rai Province.

Administration
The district is subdivided into 11 subdistricts (*tambon*), which are further subdivided into 108 villages (*muban*). Wiang Phrao is a township (*thesaban tambon*), which covers parts of *tambon* Wiang and the whole Thung Luang. There are further 9 Tambon administrative organizations (TAO).
Source (edited): "http://en.wikipedia.org/wiki/Phrao_District"

Samoeng District

Samoeng (Thai: สะเมิง) is a district (*amphoe*) of Chiang Mai Province in northern Thailand.

Geography
Neighboring districts are (from the north clockwise) Mae Taeng, Mae Rim, Hang Dong, Mae Wang, Mae Chaem and Galyani Vadhana of Chiang Mai Province and Pai of Mae Hong Son Province.

History
The district was originally created in 1902. At first it was a minor district (*King Amphoe*), which was upgraded to a full district in 1908. 1938 it was again downgraded to a minor district, and upgraded back to a full district 1958.

Administration
The district is subdivided into 5 subdistricts (*tambon*), which are further subdivided into 45 villages (*muban*). Samoeng Tai is a subdistrict municipality (*thesaban tambon*), which covers parts of *tambon* Samoeng Tai. There are further 4 Tambon administrative organizations (TAO).
Source (edited): "http://en.wikipedia.org/wiki/Samoeng_District"

San Kamphaeng District

San Kamphaeng (Thai: สันกำแพง) is a district (*amphoe*) of Chiang Mai Province in northern Thailand.

Geography
San Kamphaeng borders the districts (from west clockwise) Saraphi, Mueang Chiang Mai, San Sai, Doi Saket, Mae On of Chiang Mai Province and Ban Thi of Lamphun Province.

History
The district goes back to the *Kwaeng* Mae Om, which was established in 1902. In 1923 the district was renamed to San Kampaeng.

Economy
San Kamphaeng is famous for its many silk factories. Along the road from Chiang Mai to San Kamphaeng are many handicraft shops selling traditional Thai items to tourists, like the umbrellas of Bo Sang.

Administration
The district is subdivided into 10 sub-districts (*tambon*), which are further subdivided into 100 villages (*muban*). There are two townships (*thesaban tambon*) - San Kamphaeng covers parts of *tambon* San Kamphaeng and Chae Chang, and the whole *tambon* Sai Mun; and Ton Pao covers the whole *tambon* Ton Pao. There are further 8 Tambon administrative organizations (TAO). Numbers 7-9,14,15 are tambon which now belong to King Amphoe Mae On.
Source (edited): "http://en.wikipedia.org/wiki/San_Kamphaeng_District"

San Pa Tong District

San Pa Tong (Thai: สันป่าตอง) is a district (*amphoe*) of Chiang Mai Province in northern Thailand.

Geography
Neighboring districts are (from the southwest clockwise) Doi Lo, Mae Wang, Hang Dong of Chiang Mai Province, Mueang Lamphun and Pa Sang of Lamphun Province.

History
Originally named Ban Mae, it was renamed to San Pa Tong in 1939.

Administration
The district is divided into 11 subdistricts (*tambon*), which are further subdivided into 121 villages (*muban*). There are two townships (*thesaban tambon*) - San Pa Tong covers parts of *tambon* Yu Wa, Makham Luang and Thung Tom; and Ban Klang which covers parts of Ban Klang, Tha Wang Phrao, Makham Luang and Ma Khun Wan. There are further 11 Tambon administrative organizations (TAO).
Missing numbers are *tambon* which now form Mae Wang district.
Source (edited): "http://en.wikipedia.org/wiki/San_Pa_Tong_District"

San Sai District

San Sai (Thai: สันทราย) is a district (*amphoe*) in the central part of Chiang Mai Province in northern Thailand.

History
In the rainy season, the Ping and Khao rivers bring a lot of sand to accumulate at the area of the rivers join together year by year. It happens a big sand dune. Now the area is the location of San Sai district office. When the government created the district in this area on October 20, 1897, they selected name San Sai. San means Dune and Sai means Sand.

Geography
Neighboring districts are (from the north clockwise) Mae Taeng, Doi Saket, San Kamphaeng, Mueang Chiang Mai and Mae Rim and of Chiang Mai Province.

Administration
The district is subdivided into 12 sub-districts (*tambon*), which are further subdivided into 116 villages (*muban*). There are two townships (*thesaban tambon*) - San Sai Luang covers parts of *tambon* San Sai Luang, San Sai Noi, San Phranet and Pa Phai; and Mae Cho parts of *tambon* Nong Chom, Nong Han and Pa Phai. There are further 10 Tambon administrative organizations (TAO).
Source (edited): "http://en.wikipedia.org/wiki/San_Sai_District"

Saraphi District

Saraphi (Thai: สารภี) is a district (*amphoe*) of Chiang Mai Province, northern Thailand.

Geography
Saraphi borders the districts (from west clockwise) Hang Dong, Mueang Chiang Mai, San Kamphaeng of Chiang Mai Province, Mueang Lamphun of Lamphun Province.

History
The district was established in 1891,

then named Yang Noeng (ยางเนิ้ง). In 1927 it was renamed to Saraphi.

Administration
The district is subdivided into 12 sub-districts (*tambon*), which are further subdivided into 105 villages (*muban*). Yang Noeng is a township (*thesaban tambon*) which covers parts of the *tambon* Yang Noeng, Saraphi and Nong Phueng. The township Saraphi covers further parts of *tambon* Saraphi. There are further 10 Tambon administrative organizations (TAO).
Source (edited): "http://en.wikipedia.org/wiki/Saraphi_District"

Wiang Haeng District

Wiang Haeng (Thai: เวียงแหง) is a district (*amphoe*) in the northern part of Chiang Mai Province, northern Thailand.

History
The area of *tambon* Wiang was very far from Chiang Dao district center. The government separated *Tambon* Mueang Haeng and Piang Luang to create a minor district (*King Amphoe*) on May 5, 1981. It was upgraded to a full district on November 4, 1993.

Geography
Neighboring districts are (from the northeast clockwise) Chiang Dao of Chiang Mai Province, Pai of Mae Hong Son Province and Shan State of Myanmar.

Administration
The district is subdivided into 3 subdistricts (*tambon*), which are further subdivided into 26 villages (*muban*). There are no municipal (*thesaban*) areas, and 3 Tambon administrative organizations (TAO).
Source (edited): "http://en.wikipedia.org/wiki/Wiang_Haeng_District"

Wat Aranyawiwake

Wat Aranyawiwake (Thai script: วัดอรัญญวิเวก), also known as **Wat Ban Pong** (Thai script: วัดบ้านปง) is a monastery ("Wat") in the Thai Forest Tradition of the Theravada lineage of Buddhism located in Mae Taeng, Chiang Mai Province, northern Thailand. Phra Ajahn Plien Panyapatipo is the current abbot of Wat Aranyawiwake, where he resided since 1966. Wat Aranyawiwake was established and named by Luang Pho Mun Bhuridatta, the "father" of the current tradition of forest meditation monastics.

The Monastery
In the past, Wat Aranyawiwake was originally an old monastic residence, established by a group of people from various families in Intakhin Subdistrict, Mae Taeng District, Chiang Mai Province. They all had deep interest and faith in Buddhism.

They resolved to seek and invite virtuous monks, who were meditation masters, to reside in the village in order for them to hear the teaching of the Buddha. Later on, they heard of a monk who practiced meditation and stopped by a Wat in Mae Taeng District, so they invited the Venerable Ajahn Mun Bhuridatta. Venerable Ajahn Mun accepted the invitation and gathered a group of faithful disciples, to seek an appropriate place for practice of meditation. They searched for four days and Venerable Ajahn Mun found this place.

Upon the end of the rain retreat, his Venerable Ajahn Mun and the disciples decided to leave the place to continue their austere practice. His Venerable Ajahn Mun told the faithful followers, who attended him in Ban Pong, that he had named this place "Aranyawiwake monastic residence", The name of this monastic residence "Aranyawiwake" was given by Venerable Ajahn Mun.
Source (edited): "http://en.wikipedia.org/wiki/Wat_Aranyawiwake"

Wat Doi Mae Pang

Wat Doi Mae Pang (Thai: วัดดอยแม่ปั๋ง) is a Buddhist temple in Phrao district, Chiang Mai Province, northern Thailand. It is some 75 kilometres from the city Chiang Mai on route 1001 towards Phrao.

Its greatest claim to fame is that it was the home to Luang Por Waen Sujinno, a famous and revered monk, from 1962 until his death in 1985. Many of the buildings are of wooden construction, including the viharn and a hermit's cell called Rong Yang Giled or Rong Fai. Relics of Luang Por Waen Sujinno include his dwelling hut, a picture in the pavilion that shows him meditating, and a square-shaped, spire-roofed museum with his ashes, a wax model of the monk, and his person effects.
Source (edited): "http://en.wikipedia.org/wiki/Wat_Doi_Mae_Pang"

Baan Haw Mosque

Hedaytul Islam (Baan Haw) Mosque (Chinese: 王和清真寺; pinyin: *wánghéqīngzhēnsì*, Thai:

มัสยิดเฮดายาตุลอิสลามบ้านฮ่อ), located at Night Bazaar in Chiang Mai, is one of the biggest mosques in the province, and also one of the seven Chinese mosques in Chiang Mai.

History

It was first built in nineteenth century by a group of Chinese people, called Chin Ho or Hui, mostly came from Yunnan. The present-day buildings were built later, with an Arabic style rather a Chinese style, except in front of the prayer hall, there is a Chinese word, "清真寺",which means a mosque.

Education

Every Saturday and Sunday, there is a class for young local Muslims, beginning around 8 O'clock to the noon prayer (dhuhr). The mosque also receives 20 students each year for parents who can't afford to send their children to a government school. However, most of them are from the other part of the country, rather in Chiang Mai. The students are both Chinese and non-Chinese Muslims.

Three Chinese letters, "清真寺", which mean mosque.

The left minaret of Ban Hoe Mosque

The main building
Source (edited): "http://en.wikipedia.org/wiki/Baan_Haw_Mosque"

Badminton at the 1995 Southeast Asian Games

A **badminton** tournament was held at the **1995 Southeast Asian Games** in Chiang Mai.
Source (edited): "http://en.wikipedia.org/wiki/Badminton_at_the_1995_Southeast_Asian_Games"

Bhubing Palace

File:Dsc.jpg

Bhubing Palace (Thai: พระตำหนักภูพิงคราชนิเวศน์; also spelled *Phuping* or *Phuphing*) is a Royal Residence located Doi Buak Ha, Muang District, Chiang Mai Province, Thailand. It was built in 1961 to accommodate the royal family during state visits to the north of the country. There is also a guesthouse for receiving foreign dignitaries. It is built in the mountains overlooking Chiang Mai, to take advantage of the cool mountain air. The rose gardens are particularly famous (Suan Suwaree), and many flowers are grown here that could not otherwise be grown in Thailand.

Phra Tamnak Bhubing Rajanives was built in central Thai architectural style called "Reun Mu" (Group of Houses). The building sits on stilts. The upper floor is the royal residential area while the ground floor houses the royal entourage. The building master plan was designed by Prince Samaichalerm Kridagara while the building was designed by Mom Rachawongse Mitrarun Kasemsri. The construction of the Palace was undertaken by the Crown Property Bureau, under the supervision of Prince Samaichalerm Kridagara, assisted by Mom Rachawongse Mitrarun Kasemsri and Mr.Pradit Yuwapukka. General Luang Kampanath Saenyakorn, the Privy Councilor was assigned to lay foundation stones on 24 August 1961 at 10:49 hrs.

The Construction took 5 months to complete. The first royal visitors to stay at the Palace were King Federick the Ninth and queen lngrid of Denmark on their royal visit to Thailand in January 1962

The palace is open to the public, except when the royal family is in residence (usually January to March).
Source (edited): "http://en.wikipedia.org/wiki/Bhubing_Palace"

Chiang Mai

Chiang Mai (Thai: เชียงใหม่ , IPA: [tɕʰiəŋ màj], Northern Thai: IPA: [tɕiəŋ màj]) sometimes written as "Chiengmai" or "Chiangmai", is the largest and most culturally significant city in northern Thailand, and is the capital of Chiang Mai Province. It is located 700 km (435 mi) north of Bangkok, among the highest mountains in the country. The city is on the Ping river, a major tributary of the Chao Phraya river.

In recent years, Chiang Mai has become an increasingly modern city and has been attracting over 5 million visitors each year, of which between 1.4 million and 2 million are foreign tourists (depending on the year). Chiang Mai gained prominence in the political sphere in May 2006, when the Chiang Mai Initiative was concluded here be-

tween the ASEAN nations and the "+3" countries (China, Japan, and South Korea). Chiang Mai is one of three Thai cities contending to host the World Expo 2020. It has also recently positioned itself to become a Creative City and is considering to apply for Creative City Status with UNESCO.

Chiang Mai's historic importance is derived from its strategic location on the Ping river and major trading routes. The city has long been a major center for handcrafted goods, umbrellas, jewelry (particularly silver) and woodcarving.

While officially the city (*thesaban nakhon*) of Chiang Mai only covers most parts of the Mueang Chiang Mai district with a population of 160,000, the urban sprawl of the city now extends into several neighboring districts. This Chiang Mai Metropolitan Area has a population of nearly one million people, more than half the total of Chiang Mai Province.

The city is subdivided into four wards (*khwaeng*): Nakhon Ping, Srivijaya, Mengrai, and Kawila. The first three are on the west bank of the Ping River, and Kawila is located on the east bank. Nakhon Ping district comprises the north side of the city. Srivijaya, Mengrai, and Kawila consist of the west, south, and east respectively. The city center—within the city walls—is mostly with Srivijaya ward.

History

Wat Chiang Man, the oldest Buddhist temple in the city

The north-western corner of the city wall

King Mengrai founded the city of Chiang Mai (meaning "new city") in 1296, and it succeeded Chiang Rai as capital of the Lanna kingdom. The ruler was known as the Chao. The city was surrounded by a moat and a defensive wall, since nearby Burma was a constant threat. With the decline of the Lannathai kingdom, the city lost importance and was often occupied either by the Burmese or Thais from Ayutthaya. Because of the Burmese wars that culminated in the fall of Ayutthaya in April 1767, Chiang Mai was abandoned between 1776 and 1791. Lampang then served as the capital of what remained of Lannathai. Chiang Mai formally became part of Siam in 1774 by an agreement with Chao Kavila, after the Thai King Taksin helped drive out the Burmese. Chiang Mai then slowly grew in cultural, trading and economic importance to its current status as the unofficial capital of northern Thailand, second in importance only to Bangkok.

The inhabitants speak Kham Muang (also known as Northern Thai or Lanna) among themselves, though Central Thai is used in education and is understood by everyone. English is used in hotels and travel-related businesses and many educated people speak English. The Kham Muang alphabet is now studied only by scholars, and Northern Thai is commonly written with the standard Thai alphabet.

The modern municipality dates to a sanitary district (*sukhaphiban*) that was created in 1915. This was upgraded to a municipality (*thesaban*) on March 29, 1935, as published in the *Royal Gazette*, Book No. 52 section 80. First covering just 17.5 km (7 sq mi), the city was enlarged to 40.216 km (16 sq mi) on April 5, 1983.

Climate

Chiang Mai has a tropical wet and dry climate (Koppen *Aw*), tempered by the low latitude and moderate elevation, with warm to hot weather year-round, though nighttime conditions during the dry season can be cool and are much lower than daytime highs.

A panoramic view of the city of Chiang Mai during the rainy season, September 2010

Emblem

The city emblem depicts the chedi at Wat Doi Suthep in its center. Below it are clouds, representing the moderate climate in the mountains of northern Thailand. There is a naga, the mythical snake said to be the source of the Ping River, and rice stalks, which refer to the fertility of the land.

Religious sites

Fireworks during the extended Loi Krathong festivities in Chiang Mai over Wat Phantao

The *chedi* at Wat Phrathat Doi Suthep

The Baan Haw Mosque.

Chiang Mai has over 300 Buddhist temples (called "wat" in Thai). These include:

Wat Phrathat Doi Suthep, the city's most famous temple, stands on Doi Suthep, a hill to the north-west of the city. This temple dates from 1383. By tradition, its site was chosen by placing a relic of the Lord Buddha on an elephant's back and letting it roam until it trumpeted, then circled, and finally laid down and died. The temple's location provides superb views on a clear day.

Wat Chiang Man, the oldest temple in Chiang Mai, dates from the 13th century. King Mengrai lived here during the construction of the city. This temple houses two important and venerated Buddha figures, the marble Phra Sila and the crystal Phra Satang Man.

Wat Phra Singh is located within the city walls, dates from 1345 and offers an example of classic northern Thai style architecture. It houses the Phra Singh Buddha, a highly venerated figure brought here many years ago from Chiang Rai. Visitors can also take part in meditation classes here.

Wat Chedi Luang was founded in 1401 and is dominated by a large Lanna style *chedi* which took many years to finish. An earthquake damaged the *chedi* in the 16th century and only two-thirds of it remains.

Wat Chet Yot is located on the outskirts of the city. Built in 1455, the temple hosted the Eighth World Buddhist Council in 1977.

Wiang Kum Kam is at the site of an old city on the southern outskirts of Chiang Mai. King Mengrai lived there for ten years before the founding of Chiang Mai. The site includes many ruined temples.

Wat Umong is a forest and cave wat in the foothills in the west of the city, near Chiang Mai University. Wat U-Mong is known for its *fasting Buddha*, representing the Buddha at the end of his long and fruitless fasting period before he gained enlightenment. It illustrates a canonical text in which Buddha admonished his monks not to fall into self-torture, since it is a "fruitless" as self-indulgence. Hundreds of Buddhist proverbs in both English and Thai posted on trees throughout the grounds. They were collected by a German monk who lived there in the 1980s. Ironically, only a few of the English language sayings are by the Buddha; the rest are by a Vedanta Hindu saint who inspired the earliest Theosophists!

Wat RamPoeng (Tapotaram), near Wat U-Mong, is known for its meditation center (Northern Insight Meditation Center). The temple teaches the traditional vipassana technique and students stay from 10 days to more than a month as they try to meditate at least 10 hours a day. Wat RamPoeng houses the largest collection of *Tipitaka*, the complete Theravada canon, in several Northern dialects.

Wat Suan Dok is a 14th century temple located just west of the old city-wall. It was built by the king for a revered monk visiting from Sukhothai for the rains retreat. The temple's large sala kan prian (sermon hall) is unusual not only for its size, but also because it is open on the sides instead of enclosed. There are many chedis which contain the ashes of the old rulers of Chiang Mai. The temple is also the site of Mahachulalongkorn Rajavidyalaya Buddhist University, where monks pursue their studies.

Chiang Mai has about 20 Christian churches, 13 mosques, two gurdwaras (Sikh Temples) and a Hindu temple. Of the 13 mosques, 7 belong to Chinese or Chin Haw Muslims. The gurdwaras are Siri Guru Singh Sabha and Namdhari Sikh Temple; the Hindu temple is Devi Mandir.

Culture

Thousands of Khom Fai in Mae Jo during Loi Kratong

A truckload of people after getting hit by water during Songkran in Chiang Mai

A street in Chiang Mai

Chiang Mai hosts many Thai festivals, including:
- Loi Kratong (known locally as Yi Peng): Held on the full moon of the 12th month in the traditional Thai lunar calendar, being the full moon of the 2nd month of the old Lanna calendar. In the western calendar this usually falls in November. Every year thousands of people assemble floating banana-leaf containers (*krathong*) decorated with flowers and candles onto the waterways of the city to worship the Goddess of Water. Lanna-style sky lanterns (*khom fai*), which are hot-air balloons made of paper, are launched into the air. The sky lanterns are believed to help rid the locals of troubles and are also taken to decorate houses and streets.
- Songkran: Held in mid-April to celebrate the traditional Thai new year. Chiang Mai has become one of the most popular locations to visit for this festival. A variety of religious and fun-related activities (notably the good-natured city-wide water-fight) take place each year, along with parades and a Miss Songkran beauty competition.
- Chiang Mai Flower Festival: A three-day festival held during the first weekend in February each year, this event occurs when Chiang Mai's temperate and tropical flowers are in full bloom. The festivities include floral floats, parades, traditional dancing shows, and a beauty contest.
- Tam Boon Khan Dok, the Inthakin (City Pillar) Festival, starts on the day of the waning moon of the six lunar month and lasts 6–8 days. In 2009, this is May 20–27. Centered around Wat Chedi Luang where the city pillar is housed, this is a celebration of brahmic origin. Offerings are made to the city pillar as well as the many other Buddhist and Lanna-era icons. Dancing, musical performances, carnival games, and the ubiquitous Thai vendor food is present. This is a very large celebration in which the Chiang Mai citizenry participate.

Some of the museums in Chiang Mai:
- Chiang Mai City Arts and Cultural Center.
- Chiang Mai National Museum highlights the history of the region and the Kingdom of Lanna.
- Tribal Museum showcases the history of the local mountain tribes.

Chiang Mai has several universities, including Chiang Mai University, Chiangmai Rajabhat University, Rajamangala University of Technology, Payap University, Far Eastern University, and Maejo University—as well as numerous technical and teacher colleges. Chiang Mai University was the first government university established outside of Bangkok. Payap University is the first private institution in Thailand that was granted university status.

- Khantoke dinner is an old Lanna Thai tradition in Chiang Mai. It is an elaborate dinner or lunch which is offered by a host to guests at various ceremonies or parties, e.g. at weddings, housewarmings, celebrations, novice ordinations, or funerals. It can also be held for temple celebrations such as celebrations for specific buildings in a Thai temple and at Buddhist festivals such as Khao Pansa, Og Pansa, Loy Krathong, and Thai New Year (Songkran).

Nature
- The nearby national parks include Doi Inthanon, the highest mountain in Thailand, Doi Pui Suthep and Obkhan.
  - Doi Pui Suthep National Park is just outside town. From all over Chiang Mai you can see the Wat Doi Suthep Buddhist temple looking down on the town from Doi Suthep mountain, it is a favorite place to visit for tourists and locals alike. Chiang Mai hiking group organizes free weekly hikes often in the Doi Pui Suthep National Park and has a map of hiking trails on their web site.
- Elephant Nature Park: Approximately 60 km (37 mi) north of the city or about one hour drive, the Elephant Nature Park is home to approximately 30 rescued elephants. You can visit the park with options ranging from a day trip to volunteering.
- Hill-tribe tourism and trekking: A large number of tour companies offer organized treks among the local hills and forests on foot and on elephant back. Most also involve visits to the various local hill tribes. These include representatives from the Akha, Hmong, Karen, and Lisu tribes.
- Several venues located in the vicinity of Chiang Mai offer zip-line tours and canopy walks.

Night-life
The Chiang Mai night-life is not as concentrated or outrageous as Bangkok's infamous Nana Plaza area or Pattaya. There are many relaxing bars, several discotheques, live music venues and one street with hostess bars which cater to tourists, located along Loi Kroh Road. It includes a walk-in arcade with a Muay Thai boxing ring near the Imperial Mae Ping Hotel. The city maintains its liberal, laid back attitude with several areas and venues that accommodate the gay and lesbian scene. The Chiang Mai night-life is lively and goes well into the small hours. Bars and late-night restaurants are located all over the city, but many can be found on either side of the moat's eastern flank (in the Thapae Gate area), with some excellent live music venues along the Ping River near Nawarat Bridge, along Immanent road in the western part of the city or in the vicinity of the night bazaar. At the Galare Centre, there is a free display of

Thai cultural dancing and music. There is also a cluster of bars, American franchise fast food and coffee outlets together with more eclectic restaurants near the intersection of Chang Klan and Loi Kroh Road. Karaoke lounges (which are undoubtedly a national and indeed Asian obsession) can be found all over the city. Many are found at Chiang Mai Land Road, and some very large establishments along the length of Chang Klan Road, extending south from the famed night bazaar. There are only a couple of go-go bars in Chiang Mai.

Chiang Mai Night Safari was established as evening and night tourist attraction.

Shopping, massage and cookery

- Shopping: Chiang Mai has a large and famous night bazaar for arts, handicrafts, and imported products of all descriptions, and a number of large, well-appointed modern shopping centres. The night bazaar alone sprawls along several city blocks along footpaths, inside buildings and temple grounds, and in open squares. A handicraft and food market opens every Sunday afternoon till late on Rachadamnoen Road, the main street in the historical centre, which is closed to motorised traffic. Every Saturday evening a handicraft market is held along Wua Lai road, Chiang Mai's silver street on the south-side of the city beyond Chiang Mai gate, and which is then also closed to motorized traffic. Both Saturday and Sunday events attract many local residents and tourists.
- Visitors seeking bargains can also find a thriving second hand "Thieves" market with lots of interesting stalls under shady trees across the river to the east of the city beginning at the intersection of Kaeo Nawarat and Ratanakosin Roads.
- Thai massage: The back streets and main thoroughfares of Chiang Mai have an abundance and variety of massage parlours which offer anything from quick, simple, face and foot massages, to month-long courses in the art of Thai massage.
- Thai cookery: A number of Thai cooking schools have their home in Chiang Mai (see also Thai food).
- Central Plaza Chiang Mai Airport: An ultra-modern air-conditioned shopping mall located 10 minutes from the city centre near the international airport of Chiang Mai has the full array of western and Thai fashion, electronics, food franchises, coffee shops, a large Cineplex with optional luxury seating and 3D screens showing the latest release western movies in English plus fine examples from the burgeoning Thai movie industry with an adjacent thriving low cost food hall and restaurants.
- A focal point of the Plaza is the unique Lanna style Northern Village shopping section featuring high quality local clothing handicrafts and furnishings over three floors. On the lower floor is a mouth watering array of typical Northern Thai Cuisine.
- Kad Suan Kaew Central mall, located on Huay Kaew road just 100–200 m from the old city moat, being even bigger than Central Airport Plaza, offers similar range of services and shopping/entertainment options.
- For IT shopping, there's Pantip Plaza (much smaller than the one in Bangkok) just south of Night Bazaar, as well as Computer Plaza near the northern moat and IT City department store in Kad Suan Kaew mall.
- As a major Thai city, Chiang Mai has hypermarkets of all major networks represented in Thailand, including two Tesco Lotus Supercenters (as well as three much smaller Tesco Lotus Express supermarkets), two Big C's, one Carrefour, and one Makro. Those are located on highways in the peripheral areas of the city and are highly popular among locals and expats.

Transportation

Songthaew on Wualai Road in Chiang Mai

Tuk-tuks waiting for passengers near Tapae Gate in Chiang Mai

Bus, train and air connections serve Chiang Mai well. A number of bus stations link the city to central and northern Thailand. The Central Chang Pheuak terminal (north of Chiang Puak Gate) provides local services within Chiang Mai province and the Chiang Mai Arcade bus terminal north-east of the city (requires Songthaew or tuk-tuk ride, see below) provides services to over 20 other destinations in Thailand including Bangkok, Ayutthaya, and Phitsanulok. There are several services a day from Chiang Mai Arcade terminal to Bangkok (a 10–12 hour journey).

The state railway operates 14 trains a day to Chiang Mai Station from Bangkok. Most journeys run overnight and take approximately 12–15 hours. Most trains offer first-class (private cabins) and a second-class (seats fold out to make sleeping berths) service. A third-class offered is the most economical service, its lack of comfort makes it unsuitable for many tourists.

To get to cities such as Mae Hong

Son or Chiang Rai a plane or bus must be used. No trains are available to cities north of Chiang Mai.

Chiang Mai International Airport receives up to 28 flights a day from Bangkok (flight time about 1 hour 10 minutes) and also serves as a local hub for services to other northern cities such as Chiang Rai, Phrae and Mae Hong Son. International services also connect Chiang Mai with other regional centres, including Hong Kong (China), Jinghong (China), Kaohsiung (Taiwan), Kuala Lumpur (Malaysia), Kunming (China), Luang Phrabang (Laos), Mandalay (Myanmar), Manila (Philippines), Seoul (Korea), Siem Reap (Cambodia), Singapore (Singapore), and Taipei (Taiwan).

The local preferred form of transport is personal motorbike and, increasingly, private car. In recent years, the number of private vehicles on the road has begun to result in traffic congestion in major arteries during peak travel times. Motorbikes are available for hire from many places in the city, and tourists take advantage of this service.

Local public transport is provided in four forms: tuktuks, songthaews, less frequently rickshaws and the recently re-launched, though infrequent, Chiang Mai Bus service. Local Songthaew fare is usually 20–50 Thai baht per person for trips in and around the city. If the group of people is larger, the fare per person will be less. Tuktuk fare is usually at least 20 baht per trip (comfortable for two, but some can squeeze in four passengers); fare increases with distance. The fare is negotiable with the driver *before* boarding. Songthaews and tuktuks normally operate until about 11pm or midnight, and then become scarce and more expensive to ride. Metered taxis are available from the airport with a 50 baht airport fee paid at a counter, plus the metered charge paid to the driver (60 baht on the meter gets you into the moated area). Tipping is not expected. Chiang Mai's fledgling local bus service was relaunched in 2006. It serves routes in and around the city, although the service itself lacks the frequency and route mass as is available in other major cities. Unlike Bangkok, which has the Bangkok Metro and Bangkok Skytrain, Chiang Mai does not have rapid transit public transport infrastructure.

Air pollution

A continuing environmental problem facing Chiang Mai is the incidence of air pollution which primarily occurs for a period of several weeks up to the beginning of April. This issue has been acknowledged for some time. Back in 1996, speaking at the Fourth International Network for Environmental Compliance and Enforcement conference, which was held in Chiang Mai in that year, the then governor of Chiang Mai, Virachai Naewboonien invited guest speaker Dr. Jakapan Wongburanawatt, the Dean of the Social Science Faculty of Chiang Mai University at that time, to discuss the state of Chiang Mai air pollution efforts. Dr. Wongburanawatt stated that back in 1994, there were already increasing numbers of city residents coming to hospitals suffering from respiratory problems associated with city air pollution. The Thailand Pollution Control Department of the Ministry of Natural Resources and Environment is actively engaged in finding solutions with public awareness campaigns and other initiatives. During this period, unlike the majority of the year, air quality in Chiang Mai often remains below recommended standards with fine-particle dust levels reaching twice the standard. The northern centre of the Meteorological Department has reported that low-pressure areas from China trap forest-fire smoke in the mountains along the Thai-Myanmar border. Chiang Mai's air quality has been perceptibly deteriorating over the past ten years. This is being addressed by a number of initiatives, and in part, is often seen in cities with increasing economic growth at the expense of a strong corresponding programme to counteract the negative effects of environmental impact. The city is often shrouded in smog during this period leading up to the rainy season. Fine particulate dust levels have sometimes been tested between 190 micrograms and 243 micrograms per cubic meter. (The standard acceptable level is 120 milligrams per cubic meter.) Amongst the minor sources of particulate matter pollution in Chiang Mai is the prevalence of burning in the city, with cremations, burning garbage, or vehicular emissions from poorly maintained diesel vehicles contributing. Added to these minor causes is dust raised during building and excavations.

Main cause

A forest fire in the mountains west of Chiang Mai in Mae Hong Son Province

The majority cause of air pollution however as proven by recorded satellite imagery, is the age-old practice of burning-off undergrowth in forests in the mountainous regions, especially along the Thai-Myanmar border.

Chiang Mai's problems are exacerbated by the fact that the city, like other areas such as Los Angeles and Salt Lake City, is located in a natural geographic bowl surrounded by mountains. The result is a slowing of air movement, picking up more particulates as they are released by cars and burning trash. Also as a result of this inversion effect, as air rises in the bowl, it effectively turns over and settles back down over the city until a welcome wind shift or rainstorm cleans the air. The Thailand Pollution Control Department of the Ministry of Natural Resources and Environment is actively engaged in finding solutions to this hazardous problem and has been for several years as Chiang Mai's air quality index numbers are ever decreasing. Exacerbating this problem, one the most popular modes of convenient low-cost public transportation in Chiang Mai—as in the rest of Thailand—is provided by differently coloured pick-up

trucks called 'Songtheouw'. Red Songtheouws (Red Cars or Rod Daeng) provide passenger requested journeys whilst other colours operate on fixed routes. People ride in the back of these trucks which are equipped with diesel engines. The exhaust systems on all of these trucks are bored out in order to increase horse power which then increases the amount of carbon emissions and heavy metals which get ejected out of the back of the vehicles. As a result, the streets of Chiang Mai are increasingly difficult to ride on when using a motorcycle. It is a very common sight to see motorcyclists protecting their breathing passages as they follow these trucks. The same can be said from the famous Tuk tuks which are ubiquitous in Thailand. The city authorities are well aware of this issue and have enacted a campaign to replace all of the older, poorly tuned offending vehicles with modern yellow and blue metered passenger taxis. As these older, air quality offenders are slowly retired, it remains to be seen if the regulating bodies will be able to effect change in Chiang Mai in the face of resistance the drivers of these vehicles who have traditionally made their living in this way for many years. It should be said that Chiang Mai is not the only Thai city with this problem as Songtheow and Tuk Tuk is the major mode of low cost transportation in Thailand. Unfortunately, because of Chiang Mai's inversion effect as the result of it being situated in a geographic bowl, the carbon emissions emitted from vehicles is made an even more troubling problem.

For several years, as Chiang Mai's air quality index has become more and more troublesome, in relation to the rest of the region, the recognition of the problem has been growing locally. Doctors in Chiang Mai have been noticing an increase in people coming to see them with upper respiratory difficulties. Chiang Mai has now enacted stringent regulation of emissions standards for all vehicles. Since 2008, police sometimes set up roadblocks to test exhaust emissions on the spot and officers will enact the law to ban offending vehicles as Chiang Mai continues to work actively towards a cleaner environment.

Sister cities

-  Kunming, Yunnan, China

Gallery

Inthakhin—city pillar building, Wat Chedi Luang.

Street food at the *Sunday Evening Market*.

Selling umbrellas at the *Sunday Evening Market*.

A police tuktuk at Tapae Gate.

A street scene in Chiang Mai, showing (center right), a gate of the old city wall.

Looking south along the eastern moat of the historical city center of Chiang Mai. The road on the right is Moon Muang, on the left, Chaiya Poom.

The *Ho Trai* (library) of Wat Phra Singh

The *Sunday Evening Market* is one of the main attractions of Chiang Mai
Source (edited): "http://en.wikipedia.org/wiki/Chiang_Mai"

Chiang Mai Creative City

Chiang Mai Creative City (Thai: เชียงใหม่เมืองสร้างสรรค์) Chiang Mai Creative City is an initiative to develop Chiang Mai into a Creative City. A Creative City is a city where cultural and creative activities are an integral part of the city's economic and social functioning. The experience of other cities which have implemented such strategies has shown that they can be more successful (with meeting their development objectives) than cities which have not.

The initiative covers creative clusters but also other issues such as urban de-

velopment, education, R&D and innovation and collaboration. Some of the involved stakeholders put emphasis on the IT, software and digital content sector - since it is an important growth sector and an enabler for other sectors. Moroever, this sector also has a high potential for generating spillover effects, creating value-added, and attracting additional investment.

Existing key sectors such as tourism (e.g. medical tourism, cultural tourism, historical tourism), handicrafts (jewellry, silverware, celadon and other forms of pottery, textile, etc.), food/agro-industry, and healthcare are also targeted and can be upgraded using new designs, processes, IT, (technology based) innovation, and creative thinking.

Background

The Chiang Mai Creative City Development Committee was set up by the Governor of Chiang Mai and consists of members from the education, private and government sectors. The Governor of Chiang Mai Province, the president of Chiang Mai University, the president of Payap University, the president of North Chiang Mai University, and the US Consul General are advisors.

The Development Committee organised several activities such as a logo and website design competition and a seminar on how to develop a creative city with a guest speaker from Austin. One of the next events is with guest speaker from UNESCO to discuss how Chiang Mai could be become a UNESCO recognised Creative City.

The objective of the Development Committee are to develop a roadmap and strategy for Chiang Mai Creative City, coordinate and share information across stakeholders, coordinate and govern projects, implement and operate activities and projects, set up working committees and working teams as required.

Chiang Mai University was nominated to chair the Development Committee and to provide the secretariat and point of contact. At the present staff is allocated on a part-time and voluntary basis (by CMU).

The Development Committee is not a legal entity, but relies on its formal and informal members to support and work together. Longer-term, the Development Committee may need to institutionally developed further and become a legal entity, but is premature to conclude this now. The way of working of the Development Committee is on a consensus but also voluntary basis. This means that the Development Committee can suggest policies, projects, and activities (and if asked coordinate and govern these), but it is up to the members to implement these (and provide resources).

Vision and Mission

The timeframe for Chiang Mai Creative City needs to be long-term (15-20 years). Medium-term, the vision and objectives should align with Thailand's next national social and economic development plan (2012-2016), which will have a strong emphasis on creativity, creative economy, knowledge and innovation. Creative industries comprise 13% of total GDP (2009) and the government intends to increase this to at least 20%. Chiang Mai has an opportunity to take a significant share of this growth.

The vision may include the following aspects:

"Chiang Mai will become a recognised centre for IT, digital content, and other creative sectors, activities and talent. Technology, design, creative thinking and innovation support existing key industries as well as the social, environmental and economic objectives of the city, province and people. It is attractive as a place for living, investing, retiring, visiting, studying and working."

The mission of the Chiang Mai Creative City initiative includes

- Developing talent to better meet the needs of industry and society
- Marketing Chiang Mai as an attractive location for investment and business
- Developing the creative industries in Chiang Mai, including IT, software and digital content cluster – leverage to develop existing industries
- Develop city into a stronger growth engine and service hub for the rest of Northern Thailand
- Creating more business opportunities and jobs
- Promoting creativity (creative thinking, innovation, etc) at all levels
- Ensuring that Chiang Mai's historic and cultural heritage are preserved and that development is sustainable
- Embracing and creating benefits for all key stakeholders groups

Source (edited): "http://en.wikipedia.org/wiki/Chiang_Mai_Creative_City"

Chiang Mai Initiative

Participants of the Chiang Mai Initiative: regular ASEAN states marked light green; Plus Three states marked green

The **Chiang Mai Initiative (CMI)** is a multilateral currency swap arrangement among the ten members of the Association of Southeast Asian Nations (ASEAN), the People's Republic of China (including Hong Kong), Japan, and South Korea. It draws from a foreign exchange reserves pool worth US$120 billion and was launched on 24 March 2010.

The initiative began as a series of bilateral swap arrangements after the ASEAN Plus Three countries met on 6 May 2000 in Chiang Mai, Thailand, at an annual meeting of the Asian Development Bank. After 1997 Asian Financial Crisis, member countries started this initiative to manage regional short-term liquidity problems and to facilitate the work of other international financial arrangements and organizations like International Monetary Fund.

History

Conception

Former IMF Managing Director Horst Köhler: "Our advice [to the East Asian region] is to pursue regionalization, not in opposition to the IMF, because the IMF is a global institution, but to do it in a complementary fashion."

Finance ministers of members of the Association of Southeast Asian Nations (ASEAN), the People's Republic of China, Japan, and South Korea met on 6 May 2000 at the 33rd Annual Meeting of the Board of Governors of the Asian Development Bank (ADB) in Chiang Mai, Thailand, to discuss the establishment of a network of bilateral currency swap agreements. The proposal was dubbed the Chiang Mai Initiative and intended to avoid a future recurrence of the 1997 Asian Financial Crisis. It also implied the possibility of establishing a pool of foreign exchange reserves accessible by participating central banks to fight currency speculation. The proposal would also supplement international institutions such as the International Monetary Fund (IMF), which initiated a program to stabilize the collapsing financial system in 1997.

Early critics questioned the reasoning behind the initiative. The *Asia Times Online* wrote in an editorial published several days after the meeting, "The idea that the existence of a currency swap arrangement or the wider concept of an Asian monetary fund [...] could have prevented the Asian crisis or the worst of it, is both wrong and politically noxious." After IMF Managing Director Horst Köhler visited five Asian nations, including Thailand, in June 2000, the *Asia Times Online* denounced his endorsement of "the ill-conceived and likely never to be implemented Asean plus three [...] currency-swap plan". In a 2001 interview with the *Far Eastern Economic Review*, Köhler stated that the CMI would promote regional economic cooperation and development and that he would not oppose the formation of an Asian Monetary Union.

Expansion

As of 16 October 2009, the network consisted of 16 bilateral arrangements among the ASEAN Plus Three countries worth approximately US$90 billion. Additionally, the ASEAN Swap Arrangement had a reserves pool of approximately US$2 billion.

Multilateralization

In May 2007, at the 10th meeting of ASEAN+3 Finance Ministers the CMI further progress was agreed upon.

In February 2009, ASEAN+3 agreed to expand the fund to $120 billion up from the original level of $78 billion proposed in 2008.

During the April 2009 meeting of ASEAN finance ministers in Pattaya, Thailand, the individual contributions to be made by each member state toward the reserves pool were announced. Each of the six original ASEAN members—Indonesia, Malaysia, Singapore, the Philippines, and Thailand—agreed to contribute US$4.77 billion, while each of the remaining four members would contribute between US$30 million and US$1 billion. The ten countries were scheduled to meet their partners following the finance ministers' meeting, but the summit's cancellation due to the Thai political crisis delayed the

launch of the multilateral agreement to a later date. When leaders of the thirteen countries finally met in Bali in May, they finalized the individual contributions of China, Japan, and South Korea. This summit also added Hong Kong as a new participant, whose contribution was added to that of China though Hong Kong remained "a monetary administration on its own". Its participation raised China's total contribution to US$38.4 billion, equal to that of Japan, and South Korea, which agreed to contribute US$19.2 billion.

The Chiang Mai Initiative Multilateralisation (CMIM) Agreement was signed on 28 December 2009, and it will take effect on 24 March 2010.

Participants

Bloomberg estimated that participants of the Chiang Mai Initiative held more than US$4.1 trillion of foreign exchange reserves in 2009.

Notes

Vietnam's foreign reserves shrunk from US$23 billion at the end of 2008 to approximately US$16.5 billion in August 2009.

People's Republic of China

China holds the world's largest foreign exchange reserves, which reached US$1 trillion in November 2006. The figure doubled in the second quarter of 2009 and had risen by almost 14 times within the past decade. According to a Deutsche Bank official, "China's reserves will allow the [United States] to run a higher fiscal deficit than other nations". This deficit was caused by the U.S. government's additional spending in an effort to revive the economy from a recession. The reserves reached US$2.27 trillion in September 2009, and the country's sovereign wealth fund—the China Investment Corporation—had become more aggressive in its foreign investments.

Japan

Japan possesses the second largest foreign exchange reserves. It became the second country to reach US$1 trillion in reserves in February 2008. In contrast to China, which places "stringent" control on its currency, the Japanese government has not placed any control on the yen since 2004. The reserves reached US$1.06 trillion in October 2009.

South Korea

South Korea ranked sixth in foreign exchange reserves, which reached US$270.9 billion in November 2009. It accounted for 6.4 percent of the total ASEAN Plus Three reserves and 8 percent of the combined gross domestic product of the participating countries in 2009. *The Korea Times* wrote in an editorial that the country should act as a mediator between China and Japan, whose equal contributions meant that both "should refrain from racing for regional hegemony in the cooperative grouping".

Source (edited): "http://en.wikipedia.org/wiki/Chiang_Mai_Initiative"

Chiang Mai International Airport

Chiang Mai International Airport (IATA: **CNX**, ICAO: **VTCC**) is located in Chiang Mai, Thailand.

Chaing Mai International Airport

Chiang Mai International Airport is the major gateway to the north of Thailand. As of 2005, 10 airlines operate services and more than 2,000,000 passengers, 15,000 flights and 16,000 metric tons of cargo are handled. It is open in the evening until 01:00 to cater for night departures.

As a result of the temporary closure of Suvarnabhumi Airport in 2008 due to the protests, Chiang Mai became the alternative stop-over for China Airlines' Taipei-Europe flights and for Swiss International Airlines' Singapore-Zurich flights in the interim. On January 24, 2011, the airport became a secondary hub for Thai AirAsia.

Airlines and destinations

There are two terminals, one for domestic passengers and the other for international flights.

Source (edited): "http://en.wikipedia.org/wiki/Chiang_Mai_International_Airport"

Chiang Mai LRT

Chiang Mai LRT is the proposed light rail system project in Chiang Mai, Northern of Thailand. It is still in the planning state at present. The opening date is unknown. It was proposed by the former Prime Minister Thaksin Shinawatra, his hometown. Since he was deposed by coup, the status of this project is "shelved for now".

Source (edited): "http://en.wikipedia.org/wiki/Chiang_Mai_LRT"

Chiang Mai Metropolitan Area

The **Chiang Mai Metropolitan Area** (Thai: เขตนครเชียงใหม่และปริมณฑล) is the urban sprawl of the twin cities of city of Chiang Mai and town of Lamphun. It has an area of around 2,905.13 km² in 2 Province, 2,302.88 km² in Chiang Mai and 602.25 km² in Lamphun. There are 970,479 inhabitants in the metropolitan area. The population density is 334.06 inh/km². Compared with combined area of the two province as 24,612.90 km², 2,071,294 inhabitants and 84.15 inh/km² density. The metropolitan area cover 11.80% of whole area and 45.46% of whole population.

Administrative Division

The Metropolitan Area of Chiang Mai is located within the 8 inner amphoe (districts) of Chiang Mai province and 2 districts in Lamphun Province, northern Thailand. It has 1 City municipality, 2 town municipalities and 45 township municipalities.

Source (edited): "http://en.wikipedia.org/wiki/Chiang_Mai_Metropolitan_Area"

Chiang Mai Night Bazaar

Chiang Mai Night Bazaar or just **Night Bazaar** (Thai: ไนท์บาซาร์, *Nai Basa*) is located in the heart of the city, on the Chan Klan road, between Tha Pae and Sri Donchai roads. It is famous for its handicrafts and portrait paintings. There are also jewelry, toys, clothing and high tech items such as, CDs and DVDs. The market is one of the biggest tourist attractions in Chiang Mai. At first, the market was owned by Chinese merchants, but since it grew in size as more commercial buildings were built, it was no longer owned by a single group of people. Instead, there are many owners, and most of them are Thai.

Source (edited): "http://en.wikipedia.org/wiki/Chiang_Mai_Night_Bazaar"

Chiang Mai Night Safari

Chiang Mai Night Safari (Thai: เชียงใหม่ไนท์ซาฟารี) is the world's third nocturnal zoo and is a government nature theme park which is built to promote Chiang Mai tourism regarding to the government's policy apart from arts, cultures, traditions, and the beauty of nature which are the main fascinating tourist attractions.

Chiang Mai Night Safari was established after Night Safari in Singapore and China Night Safari in Guangzhou. Chiang Mai Night Safari is 2 times larger than Singapore's Night Safari.

History

Chiang Mai Night Safari was unofficially opened on November 18, 2005 and it was officially opened on February 6, 2006.

Zones

- **Savanna Safari Zone** is the exhibit zone mostly for animals whose habitat is in African savanna. This zone includes about 34 species and over 320 animals such as wildebeests, giraffes, white rhinoceroses, zebras etc.
- **Predator Prowl Zone** is the carnivorous animal zone which has approximately 27 species and over 200 animals such as tigers, lions, asiatic black bears, crocodiles etc.
- **Jaguar Trail Zone** is a walking trail around the 1.2 km *Swan Lake*. This zone has over 400 animals of beautiful and rare 50 species of smaller animals in an environment of enchanting flower gardens. Animals in this zone include white tigers, jaguars, capybaras, clouded leopards, fishing cats, Brazilian tapirs, squirrel monkeys, miniature horses, crowned cranes etc.

Resort

The resort at Chiang Mai Night Safari is composed of 5 houses :
- **Kum Payaa** is a one-story house located in the middle of a peaceful and beautiful forest.
- **Piroon Pana** is a group of houses and consists of 8 independent units. It is located in the middle of a peaceful and beautiful forest with all facilities.
- **Safari Doii** is a one-story house and each consists of 3-4 independent units located in the middle of a peaceful and beautiful forest with all necessities.
- **Phrueksa Sawan** is a one-story house and each consists of 3-4 independent units located in the middle of a peaceful and beautiful forest with all necessities.
- **Puang Chompoo** is a one-story house and each consists of 3-4 independent units located in the middle of a peaceful and beautiful forest with all necessities.

Gallery

Animals in Savanna Safari Zone

Zebra in Savanna Safari Zone

Rhinoceros in Savanna Safari Zone

Wrapping around Swan Lake in Jaguar Trail Zone

Source (edited): "http://en.wikipedia.org/wiki/Chiang_Mai_Night_Safari"

Chiang Mai Rajabhat University

Chiang Mai Rajabhat University is a university in the north of Thailand. It is under the Royal Thai Ministry of Education. The university was founded in 1924 as an agricultural teacher training college. In 1948, it became Chiang Mai Teachers College and offered majors in a variety of subject areas. On February 14, 1982, the year of King Rama IX's sixtieth birthday, His Majesty proclaimed Thailand's 36 teacher's Colleges to be Rajabhat Institutes; they then began offering majors and degree programmes in non-teaching fields. On March 6, 1985, His Majesty the King graciously granted the use of his royal crest as the Rajabhat Institute emblem. Rajabhat Institute Chiang Mai became Chiang Mai Rajabhat University in 2004.

Enrolment is about 10,000, and classes are divided into regular, evening and weekends. Most students come from secondary schools in northern Thailand, some even from remote areas. Chiang Mai Rachapbhat University is thus a community institute which provides a comprehensive education for local students and working people.

There are five faculties and one graduate school, employing about 500 faculty members.

There are four campuses:
- Wieng Boa, the main campus, is on Chang Puek Road, in the center of Chiang Mai.
- Mae Sa, the campus of Faculty of Management Science, is in Mae Rim District, 10 kilometers from Chiang Mai.
- Sa Luang (2,320 acres), campus of the Agricultural Center, is in Mae Rim District, 27 kilometers from Chiang Mai.
- Mae Hong Son campus, in Mae Hong Son, is the center for external services in educational area.

Faculty of Education

This faculty includes the Teaching Practicum Center, a Special Education Center and a Demonstration School for research and teaching profession resources. Presentations of local culture and academic services to communities are included in the faculty.

Faculty of Humanities and Social Science

The faculty aims to educate graduates to have good moral character and ro instill excellent academic abilities by means of participatory learning processes, research and information technology. Chinese, Japanese, Korean and Vietnamese language programs under the cooperation with international universities are offered, including student and teacher exchange programs.

Faculty of Science and technology

The faculty trains graduates in sciences and applied sciences, emphasizing effective use of technology and good moral character to assist in the development of local communities. The Science Center is a study center for local communities.

Faculty of Management Science

The Science faulty trains students in business management, economics, accounting, management science and public relations to facilitate necessary skills, knowledge, and professional ability in the business community.

Faculty of Agricultural Technology

The faulty provides education in agriculture sciences. Participatory projects, participatory learning processes and research in agricultural areas are incorporated into the creation of practical application in local communities

Graduate School

The graduate programs were established in 1995 to develop the potential of educators and members of the public and private sectors. The program supports community and national development

Source (edited): "http://en.wikipedia.org/wiki/Chiang_Mai_Rajabhat_University"

Chiang Mai University

Chiang Mai University (CMU) (Thai: มหาวิทยาลัยเชียงใหม่) is a public research university in northern Thailand founded in 1964 with a strong emphasis on engineering, scientific, and agriculture. Its instructional mission includes undergraduate, graduate, professional and continuing education offered through resident instruction. Its main

campus lies between Chiang Mai downtown and Doi Suthep in Chiang Mai, Chiang Mai Province.

The university is the first institute of higher education in Northern Thailand, and the first provincial university in Thailand. CMU recently set up the Technology Development Center for Industry (TDCI) to provide a one-stop interface with industry. It is also chairing the Chiang Mai Creative City Development Committee.

Campuses

Ang Kaew Reservoir on main campus

Sala Dharma on main campus

Chiang Mai University has four campuses, three of them in Chiang Mai and one in Lamphun, which together cover about 3,490 acres (14.1 km) of land. There are 18 housing complexes located on campus for students attending the university; 17 of them are on main campus and one in Mae Hea campus

Suan Sak Campus (main campus)

The main university campus, known as Suan Sak campus (Thai: สวนสัก) or Cherng Doi (Thai: เชิงดอย), lies about five kilometres west of the city center. Set against Doi Suthep, the campus occupies a 725-acre (2.93 km) site, bounded on three sides by main shopping streets and on the fourth by the Chiang Mai Zoo. The campus includes the University's administrative centre, the Science, Engineering, Humanities, and Social Sciences faculties, Political Science and Public Administration, Law, the Graduate School, all of the Campus Resource Facilities and Services and major sports facilities. An attractive feature of this campus is the Ang Kaew Reservoir. Constructed to supply water for the University, it is also a recreational area for campus residents and the local community. In the 1960s, the area was still forested. With conservation in mind, the University buildings were constructed between the trees, with the result that the campus still retains much of its original setting.

Suan Dok Campus

Still within the main campus, but a little closer to the city, the Health Sciences complex, the Suan Dok campus (Thai: สวนดอก), occupies a 110-acre (0.45 km) site which includes Faculties of Medicine, Associated Medical Sciences, Nursing, Dentistry and Pharmacy, and Maharaj Nakorn Chiang Mai Hospital, known locally as Suan Dok, the largest teaching hospital in Northern Thailand.

Mae Hea Campus

About 5 km south of the main campus, the 864-acre (3.50 km) Mae Hea campus (Thai: แม่เหียะ) is home to the Faculties of Veterinary Medicine and Agro-Industry. Energy Research and Development Institute (ERDI), the university center for renewable energy (mainly on biogas and biomass) and energy efficiency improvement center, moved from the main campus to Mae Hea campus since January 2009. This center is set as a national "biogas center of excellence", organizing biogas activities, especially biogas in swine farms.

Si Bua Ban Campus

The University's latest acquisition is the Si Bua Ban campus (Thai: ศรีบัวบาน) locates in Amphoe Mueang Lamphun, Lamphun Province, about 55 kilometres south of Chiang Mai, on a 1,890-acre (7.6 km) site close to the Lamphun industrial centre.

Academics

Chiang Mai University is a large, highly residential research university with a majority of enrollments coming from graduate and professional students.

Faculty

Language Institute

There are 20 faculty and 1 college in 3 disciplines.

Rankings

Chiang Mai University overall ranks in the nation are the 3rd (academia) and 5th (research) ranked by Thailand Office of the Higher Education Commission The international ranks are 81 in Asia (Quacquarelli Symonds, 2009)

Research Institutes

- Energy Research and Development Institute-Nakornping (ERDI)
- Research Institute for Health Sciences (RIHS)
- Social Research Institute (SRI)

Non-university schools

- Language Institute
- Chiang Mai University Demonstration School (K-12)

Alumni and notable people

Alumni

- Apirak Kosayothin, The Governor of Bangkok from 2004–2008
- Duaentemduang Na Chiangmai, Mayor of Chiang Mai from 2007–2008
- Jaroen Malaroj (pen-name Mala Khamchan), The S.E.A. Write award 1991 Writer
- Jaturon Chaisang, Former Deputy

- Prime Minister from 2002–2006
- Professor Dr. Kasem Wattanachai, Councilor of The Privy Council of Thailand from 2001–Present
- Krisana Kraisintu, Pharmacist and former Director of the Government Pharmaceutical Organization's Research and Development Institute
- Nidhi Eoseewong, writer and political commentator
- Samart Rajpolsit, Former Deputy Governor of Bangkok from 2004–2006
- Sompop Jantraka, activist
- Suraat Thongniramol, Deputy Undersecretary of Ministry of Interior
- Suthep Teuksuban, Deputy Prime Minister from 2008–Present
- Thawat Suntrajarn, Director-General. Department of Disease Control. Ministry of Public Health

Lecturers
- Minfong Ho, writer
- Roger A. Beaver, biologist

Source (edited): "http://en.wikipedia.org/wiki/Chiang_Mai_University"

Chiang Mai Zoo

Giant pandas in Chiang Mai Zoo.

Chiang Mai Zoo is the first commercial zoo in Northern Thailand. It is located in 100 Huay Kaew Road, Chiang Mai just north of Chiang Mai University. The zoo was established on 16 June, 1977.

It is a privately operated zoo which includes a large variety of animals. In addition, it provides two large aquariums. On 28 October 2008, an aquatic tunnel with a length of 133 metres (world's longest tunnel aquarium) was opened to the public. It also has a marine aquarium, which is the largest one in Asia.

Overall, 400 animal species are represented in the zoo including three giant pandas, 18 species of penguins and elephants. One of the giant pandas was born in Chiang Mai Zoo on May 29, 2009 and given the name Lin Bing. It is one of the few giant pandas born in captivity outside of China.

The area covers 200 acres (0.81 km). The company owned Chiang Mai Zoo Monorail takes visitors around the premises. It has 4 stations and is free of charge.

Source (edited): "http://en.wikipedia.org/wiki/Chiang_Mai_Zoo"

Chiang Mai Zoo Monorail

The **Chiang Mai Zoo Monorail** transports passengers around the Chiang Mai Zoo. The trains are air conditioned and carry 50-70 passengers. The fare is ฿100, and ฿150 for foreigners.

Source (edited): "http://en.wikipedia.org/wiki/Chiang_Mai_Zoo_Monorail"

Chiangmai F.C.

Chiangmai Football Club (Thai สโมสรฟุตบอลจังหวัดเชียงใหม่) is a Thai semi professional football club based in Chiang Mai Province, a city located in the very northern part of Thailand. The club currently plays in Thai Division 1 League.

Honours

Domestic Leagues
- Regional League Northern Division
  - **Winners (1)** : 2010

History of events of Chiangmai Football Club

As of January 2010:

Players

First team squad

As of February 28, 2011 Note: Flags indicate national team as has been defined under FIFA eligibility rules. Players may hold more than one non-FIFA nationality.

Affiliated Clubs

- ▬▬ BEC Tero Sasana

Source (edited): "http://en.wikipedia.org/wiki/Chiangmai_F.C."

Dara Academy

Dara Academy (Thai: โรงเรียนดาราวิทยาลัย), the most-enrolled school in Northern Thailand, is a private, coeducational Christian school founded by members of the Church of Christ in Thailand.

Namesake

In 1888, the school was named "Phra Racha Chaya Girls' School" after Phra Racha Chaya (พระราชชายา) Chao Dara Rasmi (ดารารัศมี), a princess from the Thipjakrathiwong dynasty of Chiang Mai. Technically, she was a "commoner" from the point of view of the Chakri dynasty, and was thus initially appointed as a Chao Chom. She was later 'ennobled' and given this particular title, which, although higher in status than Chao Chom, was still the most junior among the royal wives of King Chulalongkorn who were born princesses. In 1923 the school was re-named "Dara Academy". "Dara" means "star" in Thai language.

Royal visits

- 1925 His Majesty King Prajadhipok (Rama VII, Thai: พระปกเกล้าเจ้าอยู่หัว *Phra Pokklao Chaoyuhua*) and Queen Ramphaiphanni
- 1949 Queen Ramphaiphanni (*Somdej Phra Nangchao Ramphaiphanni Phra Boromarajininat* - สมเด็จพระนางเจ้ารำไพพรรณี พระบรมราชินี)
- 1958 His Majesty the King, Bhumibol Adulyadej

Native-speaker Program

Dara employs over 30 native speakers for its foreign language program (called NP), teaching English and Chinese. Countries represented include:

- Australia
- Canada
- China
- England
- South Africa
- United States
- New Zealand
- Ireland

Native Speaker Program website: www.dara.ac.th/np

Address

196 Kaewnawarat Rd, T. Watget, A. Muang, Chiangmai 50000
Address (Thai language): 196 ถ.แก้วนวรัฐ ต.วัดเกต อ.เมือง จ.เชียงใหม่. 50000
Source (edited): "http://en.wikipedia.org/wiki/Dara_Academy"

Darunaman Mosque

The tiles arranging in Chinese style, but also give the sense of symmetry.

Darun Aman Mosque (Thai: มัสยิดดารุลอามาน or Thai: มัสยิดบ้านฮ่อ) ,located at Isaraparb road, is the biggest mosques in Chiang Rai province. The mosque was one of many mosques in northern Thailand, built by Hui people or roughly known as Chin Haw in Thai.

Design

The new building has just opened in 27th December 2009, replacing the old one. It shows a great mixture between Chinese and Islamic architecture. The main structure is highly influenced by the Persian architecture with the Chinese decorations. The tip of the two minarets has been replaced with the small Chinese pavilion, instead of a typical islamic dome. The total cost was around 20 million Baht.

Gellery

The main gate of the praying hall

The central gate of the mosque, looking from inside

Inside the praying hall with the three chandeliers, bringing from China

Wan Muhammad Noor Matha was giving a speech in the opnning ceremony of the new building
Source (edited): "http://en.wikipedia.org/wiki/Darunaman_Mosque"

Dokmai Garden

Dokmai Garden is a private tropical botanical garden in the Hang Dong district in Chiang Mai, Thailand. The garden is located at N18° 40.634' E 98° 52.749'.

The aim of Dokmai Garden is to impart knowledge about tropical organisms in general, and monsoon gardening in particular.

The garden was developed by the Seehamongkol family in collaboration with western scientists who transformed a former longan plantation (*Dimocarpus longan*, an edible fruit) into a modern ethno-botanical garden with emphasis on fruits, vegetables, trees, and mushrooms. The garden opened in 2009 and covers 4 hectares (10 acres) and features more than 900 plant species and a number of free-living butterflies, birds, reptiles, and fish. There are multilingual informational signs (English, Japanese, Thai) throughout the garden, providing scientific names, history and information about 500 selected plants.

Dokmai Garden is a centre for seminars, excursions and courses in collaboration with local universities, amateurs and enterprises. The associated Dokmai Dogma is a forum for sharing experience on monsoon gardening.

Source (edited): "http://en.wikipedia.org/wiki/Dokmai_Garden"

Inthakin

Tam Boon Khan Dok, the Inthakin (City Pillar) Festival in Chiang Mai, Thailand, starts on the day of the waning moon of the six lunar month and lasts 6–8 days. In 2009, this is May 20-27. Centered around Wat Chedi Luang where the city pillar is housed, this is a celebration of brahmic origin. Offerings are made to the city pillar as well as the many other Buddhist and Lanna-era icons. Dancing, musical performances, carnival games, and the ubiquitous Thai vendor food is present. This is a very large celebration in which the Chiang Mai citizenry participate.

Wat Chedi Luang during Tam Boon Khan Dok - Inthakin City Pillar Festival

Wat Chedi Luang lit at night during Tam Boon Khan Dok

Offerings to Buddha image at Wat Chedi Luang during Tam Boon Khan Dok

Source (edited): "http://en.wikipedia.org/wiki/Inthakin"

Maejo University

Maejo University, also spelled **Maecho University** (Thai: มหาวิทยาลัยแม่โจ้), located in Chiang Mai Province, Thailand, is the oldest agricultural institution in the country. Founded in 1934 as the Northern Agricultural Teachers Training School, it was restructured and renamed several times until it gained the status of a full-fledged public university in 1996 and since then has been known as Maejo University.

Maejo University main campus at Chiang Mai is composed of the Faculties of Agricultural Business, Agricultural Production, Science, and Engineering and Agro-Industry. In addition to these, the university has two smaller campuses in Phrae and Chumphon.

President Thep Phongparnich was awarded Oklahoma State University's Distinguished International Alumni Award on November 12th, 2005. The two universities have formed an alliance.

Logo

Inside a ring with **Maejo** in Thai and English, the logo depicts Thailand's symbol of agriculture, the lord of rain Phra Phirune mounted on a Nāga (พระพิรุณทรงนาค). The symbol may be seen as a fountain here.

Mascot

Every centre of learning in Thailand has its Tutelary deity, and many have a Genius (mythology), but Maejo has also adopted the Pistol Pete (mascot) following President Thep's OK State's Distinguished International Alumni award.

Source (edited): "http://en.wikipedia.org/wiki/Maejo_University"

Montfort College

Montfort College is a school in Chiang Mai, Thailand.

History

The Brothers of St. Gabriel came to Chiang Mai and established Montfort Primary School in 1932 along Charoen Prathet Road on a 5-acre (20,000 m) plot of land provided by Bishop Peross from Luang Anusarn Suntorn who gave his financial support without interest. The land was located along the Ping River approximately 200 metres from the Sacred Heart Church. Montfort School officially opened its first academic year on 16 March 1932. Fr. Reunemenier was the Manager, Brother Simon the first Director, Brother Ambrosio the vice-Director and Brother Louis was responsible for the new constructions.

Montfort College opened the secondary section in 1949, started to admit girls at its Secondary Section from levels 10 to 12 in 1975 and started to admit girls at its Primary Section in 2009.

At present

Montfort College has 2 sections: Primary (Grade 1-6) and Secondary (Grade 7-12), has approximately 4,000 students and 400 teachers in the school now.

Notable alumni

- Thaksin Shinawatra (Former Prime Minister)
- Tharin Nimmanhemin (Former Finance Minister of Thailand)
- Bundit Ungrangsee (A famous conductor)
- Sukrit Wisetkaew (A famous Thai singer and actor)
- Witwisit Hirunwongkul (A famous Thai actor and singer)
- Chookiat Sakveerakul (A famous film director)

Source (edited): "http://en.wikipedia.org/wiki/Montfort_College"

North Chiang Mai University

North Chiang Mai University (NCU) (มหาวิทยาลัยนอร์ท-เชียงใหม่) is a private university in Chiang Mai, Thailand founded in 1999.

Source (edited): "http://en.wikipedia.org/wiki/North_Chiang_Mai_University"

Payap University

Payap University (Thai: มหาวิทยาลัยพายัพ) established in 1974, is a private institution founded by the Church of Christ in Thailand. Payap is a founding member of the Association of Private Higher Education Institutions in Thailand, and an active member of the Association of Christian Universities and Colleges in Asia, as well as the Association of Southeast Asian Institutions of Higher Learning.

History

Payap University has a long and rich history beginning in 1888 with the founding of the Thailand Theological Seminary. That seminary has now been integrated into Payap University as the McGilvary College of Divinity, one of eleven academic divisions comprising the university. Initially, seminary students were accepted after completing elementary school. High school graduation gradually became the pre-requisite for a seven-year bachelor of divinity (BD) course that was formally initiated in 1960. The second predecessor of Payap University was the McCormick Hospital School of Nursing, established in 1923. After first accepting students with minimal educational qualifications, in 1961 the School of Nursing made high school graduation a pre-requisite for entrance. Degrees awarded by these institutions, however, were not recognized as college degrees by the Royal Thai Government.

The Royal Proclamation of the Private Colleges Act of 1969 made private higher education legal in Thailand. The Thailand Theological Seminary and the McCormick Hospital School of Nursing initiated discussions to set up a private college. Together with representatives of the Church of Christ in Thailand, the American Presbyterian Mission, and the Disciples Division of Overseas Ministries, they formulated articles of incorporation which were submitted to the Royal Thai Government. Payap College received accreditation on 21 March 1974, and became the first private college in Thailand outside of greater Bangkok.

In its early years, Payap College operated in borrowed facilities. Originally there were two campuses, one adjacent to McCormick Hospital and the other five miles distant, a four-acre site on the west side of Chiang Mai, on which stood three residential buildings. Although initial plans called for the development of these two campus sites, it soon became evident that expansion of the four-acre western site near Chiang Mai University was impractical; skyrocketing real estate costs precluded additional land acquisition at that site. The eastern campus, opposite McCormick Hospital, strained to accommodate adequate facilities for both student and graduate nurses of the hospital and the students of the Thailand Theological Seminary. Although additional buildings on this 16-acre site would have been possible, facilities for the anticipated student body of several thousand students could not have been accommodat-

ed. The Board of Directors voted early in 1974 to proceed with acquisition of land in a more favorable location, two miles to the east of the McCormick campus. About 120 acres of low-lying land was then acquired; this site now comprises the Mae Khao campus, which serves as the main university campus. Subsequent land acquisitions have increased the size of this campus to approximately 275 acres.

In 1975, Payap engaged Metropolitan Engineering Consultants Co., Ltd., of Bangkok, a leading architectural and engineering firm, to prepare a ten-year master plan for campus development. The implementation of this plan began with the dedication of the first five buildings on the Mae Khao campus in 1982. Since then, 16 major buildings have been constructed at the Mae Khao campus. Payap also continues to offer classes on the Kaew Nawarat site where the College of Divinity, the faculty of nursing, the music department, the Christian Communications Institute, and the university archives are located.

Payap's achievements were recognized by the Royal Thai Government in 1984 when it became the first fully accredited private university in Thailand. Since then the university has continued to progress, expanding facilities to accommodate the steady growth in the student body, investing in the continuing education and training of the faculty through university support of graduate education in the US and in other countries, and adding a wide range of international programs to attract students from across Southeast Asia and from other areas of the world.

Academics

Payap is a Liberal Arts and Pre-Professional School offering 22 Thai language degrees in 12 departments

Undergraduate

- Accountancy, Finance and Banking
- Art
- Business Administration
- Communication Art
- Economics
- Law
- Music
- Nursing
- Pharmacy
- Science
- Social Science and Humanities
- Theology

International Programs (English Language)

- Computer Information Systems
- International Business Management
- International Hospitality Management
- English Communication

Graduate

- Master of Accountancy
- Master of Business Administration (MBA)
- Master of Divinity (MDIV)
- Master of Arts in Music
- Master of Law (ML)

International Programs (English Language)

- Master of Arts in Linguistics
- Master of Arts in Teaching English to Speakers of Other Languages Language (MA TESOL)
- Master of Business Administration in International Business (MBA)
- Master of Divinity

International University

Payap has an international student body with nearly 30 countries represented including the United States, China, Myanmar, France, Germany, Mexico, Japan, Pakistan, India and Thailand. Students share in common a strong English proficiency in order to perform in the English-speaking Bachelor's and Master's degree programs. Non-native English speaking students find that their English skills improve immensely during their studies at Payap due to the constant exposure to spoken and written English.

Source (edited): "http://en.wikipedia.org/wiki/Payap_University"

Rajamangala University of Technology Lanna

Rajamangala University of Technology Lanna (Thai: มหาวิทยาลัยเทคโนโลยีราชมงคลล้านนา) (RMUTL) is a science and technology university in northern Thailand. It offers Certificate (Vocational), Advanced Certificate (Vocational), undergraduate, and master's degrees.

History

RMUTL was first founded in 1957 under a royal charter granted by His Majesty the King Bhumibol adulyadaj under the name **Vocational Institute**. In 1975, it was considered a campus of the Institute of Technology and Vocational Education. In 1988 it was named **Rajamangala Institute of Technology (RIT), Northern Campus** by His Majesty the King. To serve the needs of people in Thailand and other countries and to meet international standards, RIT developed its administration structure and education management and became **Rajamangala University of Technology (RMUT)** in 2003. File:Rmutlogo.jpg

Faculty

- Faculty of Business Administration and Liberal Arts
- Faculty of Agricultural Science and Technology
- Faculty of Engineering
- Faculty of Arts and Architecture
- College of Technology and Interdisciplinary

Campuses

RMUT consists of nine universities and RMUTL itself has of six campuses in the north of Thailand:

- Chiang Mai Province
- Nan Province
- Lampang Province
- Phitsanulok Province
- Tak Province
- Chiang Rai Province

Source (edited): "http://en.wikipedia.

Roman Catholic Diocese of Chiang Mai

The (Roman Catholic) **Diocese of Chiang Mai** (*Dioecesis Chiangmaiensis*, Thai: สังฆมณฑลเชียงใหม่) in northern Thailand. It is a suffragan diocese of the archdiocese of Bangkok.

The diocese covers an area of 89,483 km², covering all of the northern provinces of Thailand (Chiang Mai, Chiang Rai, Lampang, Lamphun, Mae Hong Son, Nan, Phayao, Phrae). As of 2001, of the 5.8 million citizen 36,518 are member of the Catholic Church.

History

The diocese dates back to the Prefecture Apostolic of Chieng-Mai, which was erected on November 17, 1959. On December 18, 1965 it was elevated to a diocese.

Cathedral

Cathedral of the Sacred Heart

The principal church of the diocese is the Cathedral of the Sacred Heart (Thai: อาสนวิหารพระหฤทัย, Location 18°46′30.5″N 99°0′11.2″E). The current church was inaugurated on October 30, 1999, and is already the third cathedral of the diocese. The first Sacred Heart church was built in 1931. Shortly before the elevation to a diocese, the new, and larger, church was inaugurated on February 28, 1965.

Sacred Heart College and the kindergarten school that surround the church building were added later (2475 = 1932). Originally there were 40 students, now there are over 4,000. In the last few years an English Program has been created. This currently has just over 100 students. Each class is small, around 16 students or so, and has two teachers: A native Thai speaking subject teacher and likewise a native English speaking subject teacher. Whilst Sacred Heart College is a private school, its prices are controlled by the Government and are very much lower than international private schools in the area. Student range from pre-school up to university age. /

Bishops

- Francis Xavier Vira Arpondratana: February 10, 2009 - present
- Joseph Sangval Surasarang: October 17, 1986 - February 10, 2009 (resigned)
- Robert Ratna Bamrungtrakul: April 28, 1975 - October 17, 1986 (resigned)
- 1959-1975 the prefecture and later diocese was administrated by Bf. Lucien Bernard Lacoste, bishop of Dali.

Source (edited): "http://en.wikipedia.org/wiki/Roman_Catholic_Diocese_of_Chiang_Mai"

Royal Flora Ratchaphruek

Royal Pavilion

The **Royal Flora Ratchaphruek** was a flower festival held 1 November 2006, to 31 January 2007, in the Thai city of Chiang Mai that drew 3,781,624 visitors. It was one of the grand celebrations being hosted by the Royal Thai Government in honor of King Bhumibol, the world's longest reigning monarch.

The **Ratchaphruek** (*Cassia fistula* L.) or Golden Shower Tree is the national flower of Thailand. It is also named "Khun" or "Chaiyaphruek". The reason that the Ratchaphruek is used to symbolize the nation lies in color: its yellow blossoms match the yellow of Buddhism; furthermore, the Thai people regard yellow as the color of the King as well. Moreover, all golden shower trees bloom at the same time; this unity in flowering is felt to reflect the unity and identity of Thais.

The event was located in 80 hectares of land at the Royal Agricultural Research Center in Mae Hia sub-district, Mueang district, Chiang Mai Province in northern Thailand. The 92 days of the expo featured 30 international gardens reflecting nations such as Japan, South Korea, Belgium, Netherlands, South Africa, and Canada; more than 2.5 million trees of 2,200 species of tropical plants and flowers are presented to the world in this exhibition. The AIPH, the Association of International Horticultural Producers, gave this expo A1 status, its highest level; such an exhibition occurs only once a year throughout the world. In addition, a host country can only hold one such exhibition once a decade.

The festival included many highlights to attract tourists:
- **Gardens for the king** There were two features in this zone: one was *International gardens,* which were presented by 30 participating nations and covered 21,000 square meters; the other was *Corporate gardens*, which covered 27,475 square meters, and were presented by both Thai state enterprises, and domestic and international major corporations.
- **Ho Kham Royal Pavilion** This building featured Lanna architecture, the architectural style of northern Thailand; inside, visitors saw pictures of King Bhumibol's works and his dedication.
- **Thai Tropical Garden** The enormous 100,000-square-meter garden showcased the diversity of tropical horticulture: fruit varieties, plants, flowers, herbs, and rare plants.
- **Expo Plaza** This was the focus of the exposition's fun-filled activities, amenities, and services. Visitors were able to purchase products from the Royal Projects and authentic local products from Chiangmai such as handicrafts, paper umbrellas, and souvenirs.
- **Cultural shows** A total of 45 cultural shows from various regions of Thailand were performed here, including traditional music and dance. In addition, cultural performances from other nations were presented in this place.

The Thai government had expected an average of 20,000 visitors per day, with over 100,000 visitors on a crowded day, and 3 million visitors in total to attend the Royal Flora Ratchaphruek 2006. At the exposition's conclusion, organizers claimed that the exposition had injected 27 billion baht into the regional economy.

The Thai government has proposed transforming the site of the exposition into a permanent training center. Despite some complaints of corruption and substandard facilities, organizers believed the exposition achieved its goals of promoting tourism and developing Thai horticultural industries.

"Expo closes with ceremony of allegiance to His Majesty"

The park was open to the public in 2008 with many of the past highlights still very much in evidence, especially the fascinating international exhibits. It is thought that it will remain to stay open as a valued addition to things to do in Chiang Mai. Currently, admission is free, though this will most likely change. The park receives around 500 visitors a day at the moment, mainly Thai.

Source (edited): "http://en.wikipedia.org/wiki/Royal_Flora_Ratchaphruek"

Wiang Kum Kam

Chedi of Wat Kuu Kham

Wiang Kum Kam is the recently restored original settlement along the Ping River, predating Chiang Mai. It was flooded and abandoned more than 700 years ago; that move became more understandable in 2005, when the ancient city was flooded three separate times and the river left its banks in that area of Chiang Mai.

The main temple of the town is Wat Chedi Liam (originally: Wat Ku Kham), which is still occupied by monks.

Wiang Kum Kam Archeaological site, Chiang Mai, Thailand
Brief overview

Wiang Kum Kam is an ancient city, located in the north region of Thailand. It is in Sarapee district, Chiang Mai province which is approximately 5 kilometers from the center. According to the chronicles and archeological evidences, assume that the old city was built by King Mangrai at the first periods of the 13th century. The aimed of this founding was an establishment of a new capital after his victory over Hariphunchai kingdom, modern Lamphun. Wiang Kum Kam was flourished all long the reign of Mangrai dynasty until the late of 16 century. The old city was lost from history for many years after Chiang Mai was conquered by Mynmar, in 1558 A.D. The people who live in Wiang Kum Kam were escaped along the belligerency. Big flood was a presumption; result in the city was lost from the history. The people were moved back to this area again after it was abandoned more than 200 years with a new community, named Chang Kham village. There are a few of people know about Wiang Kum Kam story at first and the residence areas have interloped since then on. Until the years 1984, the Fine Arts department founded some evidences of the old city at Wat Kam thom then the excavating was started by Thai government. The archeological works and restoration were done and was expanded over the whole site from thenceforward. In additions, the archeological studies and some pilot projects of research have started since 1984 AD.

Reference: Charnnarong Srisuwan, Wiang Kum Kam Archeaological site, Chiang Mai, Thailand, 2011 Research : http://www.thaiarte.com/knowledge

Source (edited): "http://en.wikipedia.org/wiki/Wiang_Kum_Kam"

Chiang Mai Province

Chiang Mai (Thai เชียงใหม่) is the second-largest province (*changwat*) of Thailand, located in the north of the country. Neighboring provinces are (from northeast clockwise) Chiang Rai, Lampang, Lamphun, Tak, and Mae Hong Son. In the north it borders Shan State of Burma. Chiang Mai recently started to position itself as a Creative City (Chiang Mai Creative City) and is considering to apply to become a UNESCO Creative City.

Geography

Chiang Mai province is about 700 km from Bangkok and is situated on the Mae Ping River basin and is 300 m above sea level. Surrounded by high mountain ranges, it covers an area of approximately 20,107 km². The district is covered by many mountains, chiefly stretching in the south-north direction. The river Ping, one of the major tributaries of the Chao Phraya River, originates in the Chiang Dao mountains. The highest mountain of Thailand, the 2,565 meter high Doi Inthanon, is located in the province. Several national parks are in the district: Doi Inthanon, Doi Suthep-Pui, Mae Ping, Sri Lanna, Huay Nam Dang, Mae Phang, Chiang Dao.

The mountainous terrain is mainly jungle, parts of which are within national parks which are still fertile and verdant with plentiful flora and fauna. There are many sites and locations where tourists prefer to visit to study the lifestyle of the tribal people who live on high hills.

History

Pratat Doi Suthep, a temple in Chiang Mai

The city of Chiang Mai was capital of the Lanna Kingdom after its founding in 1296. During the same period of time as the establishment of the Sukhothai Kingdom. From then, Chiang Mai not only became the capital and cultural core of the Lanna Kingdom, it was also the centre of Buddhism in northern Thailand and King Meng Rai built innumerable temples.

In 1599 the kingdom lost its independence and became part of the Ayutthaya Kingdom. This ending the dynasty founded by King Meng Rai which had lasted for 300 years. The occupiers Burma, had a powerful Burmese influence on the architecture which can still be seen today. It was only in the late 18th century that Burma was finally defeated with the leadership of King Taksin.

In 1932 the province Chiang Mai became the second level subdivision of Thailand when the administrative unit of *Monthon Phayap*, the remains of the Lanna Kingdom, was dissolved.

Demographics

Tribe Girls

13.4% of the population on the province are members of the hill tribes, among them the Hmong, Yao, Lahu, Lisu, Akha and Karen.

Symbols

The seal of the province shows a white elephant in a glass pavilion. The white elephant is a royal symbol in Thailand, and it is depicted to remember the offering of a white elephant by King Rama II to the ruler of Chiang Mai. The pavilion symbolizes that Buddhism prospered in Chiang Mai, especially when in 1477 the teachings of Buddha, the Tripitaka, were reviewed.

The provincial flower and tree is the Flame of the Forest (*Butea monosperma*). The provincial slogan is **In the shadow of Doi Suthep mount, blessed with rice customs and traditions, beautiful wild flowers, magnificent Nakhon Phing**.

Administrative divisions

Chiang Mai is subdivided into 25 districts (*Amphoe*). The districts are further subdivided into 204 subdistricts (*Tambon*) and 1915 villages (*Muban*).

Climate

From November to February during the cool season, Chiang Mai province experiences pleasantly mild sunny weather with temperatures in the city area on average ranging between 15 Celsius at night and around 28 Celsius in daytime. At higher elevations, temperatures can sometimes dip down to freezing point at night. It doesn't snow, but sleet does occur at times.

During the hot season, lasting from March to May, temperatures especially in the city are high, rising into the high 30s.

The rainy season in the north is from June to October.

Transportation

Chiang Mai Train Station

Car Chiang Mai is on Highway 11 (super highway Rd.). Cars can be hired in the provincial capital.
Train Chiang Mai is the terminal station on the northern railway route.
Songthaew Songthaews (passenger pick-up vehicles) are a common mode of transport in both rural and urban areas.
Samlor Samlors (rickshaws) can be found in the main areas.
Tuk-tuk Tuk-tuks are popular with both locals and tourists for short distances.
Bus service Chiang Mai is easily accessible by a multitude of air-conditioned and non air-conditioned buses from Bangkok and all other northern provincial capitals. For travel within the province itself there are older non air-conditioned buses.
Bicycle & Motorbike Both forms of transport can be hired in the provincial capital.
Air Chiang Mai International Airport (CNX) is one of the seven international airports under the responsibility of the Airports of Thailand Public Company Limited (AOT). As Chiang Mai International Airport is the major gateway to the scenic beauty and rich culture of northern Thailand, it plays an important role in promoting travel and tourism throughout the northern region. Today, 14 airlines service the airport and more than 3,000,000 passengers, 15,000 flights and 16,000 tons of cargo are handled at this airport.

Tourism

Chiang Mai province for years now has been the tourist hub of the north and one of Thailand's most important tourist destinations. .It is considered one of the most scenic provinces in the country due to its mountain ranges, valleys, flora and fauna. Unlike most of Thailand, the climate in the north and especially Chiang Mai is cool, fresh and misty.

Attractions

Doi Suthep-Doi Pui National Park (อุทยานแห่งชาติดอยสุเทพ-ปุย) The park consists of forests and mountain ranges. Major mountains include Doi Suthep, Doi Buak Ha, and Doi Pui. This is a main source of tributaries and streams in Chiang Mai. Sacred places, religious attractions and historical sites are located in the park complex.
Walking Street Chiang Mai municipality has organized, since 2006, the Chiang Mai Sunday Evening Walking Street at the Three Kings Monument Courtyard. It has turned into a thriving Sunday evening market which now encompasses nearly the whole of Rachadamnoen road (the main road of the old city), many of its side streets and the square in front of Thapae gate. It is renowned for the locally made handicrafts. In addition, Chiang Mai also organises a Saturday Evening Walking Street on Woa Lai road which runs from Chiang Mai gate, on the south side of the old city, towards the airport.
Chiang Mai Zoo (สวนสัตว์เชียงใหม่) is located next to Huai Kaeo Arboretum. It is a large zoo, which occupies the lower forested slopes of Doi Suthep Mountain. The zoo contains more than 200 types of Asian and African mammals and birds.
Doi Inthanon National Park (อุทยานแห่งชาติดอยอินทนนท์): at 2,565 m, Doi Inthanon is Thailand's highest mountain and one of the coolest peaks. Besides the actual mountain itself, there are a variety of other attractive locations such as Mae Ya, Wachirathan and Siriphum waterfalls and Bori Chinda Cave.
Pang Chang Mae Sa: The elephant shows are a demonstration of the elephants' abilities in log-hauling. After the end of the performance, visitors are able to have a go at riding an elephant.
Wat Phra Singh (วัดพระสิงห์วรวิหาร), houses the revered Phra Phuttha Sihing Buddha (พระพุทธสิหิงค์) image cast in Subduing Mara. The Buddha image is now enshrined in Viharn Lai Kham. The temple compound includes the lovely Viharn Lai Kham featuring exquisite woodcarvings and northern-style murals paintings, a magnificent scriptural repository with striking bas relief, and a circular stupa (in Lankan bell shape).
Mae Sa Waterfall (น้ำตกแม่สา) The famous 8-tiered waterfall in Amphoe Mae Rim occupies a natural setting among towering trees, covered with a lovely breeze all year round.
Night Bazaar: Every evening the center of the provincial city holds one of the provinces biggest markets, selling a huge variety of goods to tourists, both foreign and Thai. The market is 3 blocks long and is surrounded by restaurants, cafes and travel agents.
Chiang Mai Night Safari: The world's third nocturnal zoo and is a government nature theme park which is built to promote Chiang Mai tourism regarding to the government's policy apart from arts, cultures, traditions, and the beauty of nature which are the main fascinating tourist attractions.

Entertainment/Activities

The city of Chiang Mai has a wide variety of activities.
Elephant Show The show begins with elephants bathing to cool themselves then mahouts would place a log harness on their backs. Finally, elephants will demonstrate their forestry skills. Elephant riding and rafting are the most popular activities. Some of the Elephant training centers are:
- Pang Chang Mae Taeng (ปางช้างแม่แตง)
- Chiang Dao Elephant Training Centre (ศูนย์ฝึกช้างเชียงดาว)
- Pang Chang Mae Sa (ปางช้างแม่สา)
- Pang Chang Pong Yaeng (ปางช้างโป่งแยง)

Mountain Biking Mountain biking is done on several routes in Chiang Mai including around the old city moats.
Homestay at Ban Mae Kampong The village is situated in a mountainous area with jungle surroundings. Nearby attractions include waterfalls, a cotton weaving village and the Huai Hong

Khrai Royal Agricultural Station.

Hilltribes Trekking Of particular interest to most are the six major hilltribes which inhabit the Northern Highlands. The largest group is Karen, followed by the Meo, Lahu, Yao, Akha and Lisu. They share animism beliefs and honour numerous forest and guardian spirits. Each tribe has distinctive ceremonial attire, courtship rituals, games, dances, agricultural customs, languages or dialects, aesthetic values and hygienic habits.

Bamboo Rafting-Whitewater Rafting Bamboo Rafting along the Mae Taeng River (ล่องแพลำน้ำแม่แตง) is very popular because the river zigzags along the valleys. The river tide is not too rough and the surroundings on both sides are admirable.

Cruising along the Ping River Maenam Ping is the main river in Chiang Mai. While cruising, people can witness the atmosphere of Chiang Mai, as well as the local lifestyle on both sides of the Ping River.

Artificial Rock Climbing Artificial Rock Climbing (ไต่หน้าผาจำลอง) can be practised at the Peak Rock Climbing Plaza.

Golf Courses Due to the pleasant natural surroundings and climate, Chiang Mai is popular for playing golf. There are many courses in the province.

Spa Spa treatment in Chiang Mai includes both traditional remedies and healing arts alongside modern techniques. This treatment, in terms of service available, has escalated over the past few years and there are now innumerable locations offering spa service – often including a Jacuzzi and steam bath.

Shopping Shopping in Chiang Mai is one of the most popular activities of the region. Besides the usual abundance of shopping malls and department stores, there is a huge variety of local markets. The Night Bazaar in downtown Chiang Mai is the most popular location for shopping.

Local Products

Chiang Mai is the center of handicrafts with a variety of antiques, silver jewellery, and embroidery, Thai silks and cottons, basketry, celadon, silverware, furniture, lacquerware, woodcarvings and parasols. Major Chiang Mai products include:

- **Cottons & Silks**
- **Umbrellas/ Parasols** - These are inextricably associated with Bo Sang where villagers have been engaged in their manufacture for at least 200 years. All materials, silks, cottons, Sa paper (manufactured from the bark of the mulberry tree) and bamboo are produced or found locally.
- **Silverware** - Traditional skills and a guaranteed content of at least 92.5% pure silver invest bowls, receptacles and decorative items.
- **Lacquerware** - This decorative are enhanced items made of wood, bamboo, metal, paper and baked clay, in the form of receptacles, ornaments and various souvenirs.
- **Furniture/ Woodcarving** - Major woods and materials include teak, rosewood and rattan. Items may be unadorned or, especially with teak and rosewood, carved in traditional or modern designs. Woodcarving is a traditional northern Thai art featured in numerous temples. In recent years, woodcarving has increasingly embellished furniture, gracing screens, chairs, tables, beds, figurines, carved elephant indeed anything bearing a wooden surface large enough to be carved.
- **Hilltribe Products** - These include silver ornaments, such as bracelets, necklace, pendants and pipes of intricate design, and embroidered items including tunics, jackets, bags, purses, caps and dress lengths.
- **Gold Plated Orchids & Butterflies** - Orchids and butterflies are preserved and plated with 24-carat gold to create unusual gift items such as necklace pendants, hairpins and earrings.
- **Pottery** - Chiang Mai is the major centre of Thailand's pottery industry. Prized items include high-fired celadon which is produced in many forms, including dinner sets, lamp bases and decorative items.
- **Sa (Mulberry) Paper Products**: Chiang Mai is also famous for its Sa paper products a handmade, multi-purpose natural fiber. Sa products that come in different, distinctive designs include cards, notebooks, stationery, boxes, bags, photo frames, lanterns, gift wrapping paper, etc.

Nightlife

For those who love nothing more than a decent night on the town, then Chiang Mai has one of the land's funkiest nightlife. Types of nightlife available include:

- Discos are popular with the younger trendier crowd..
- Live music pubs/restaurants playing either Thai folk music and/or international pop classics.
- Karaoke clubs can be found all around..
- Barbecues are large open-air restaurants which play music and serve alcohol..
- "Bar Beers" are popular with foreign male tourists..
- Thai Pubs are not like Western ones, they are usually huge..
- Western pubs serving draft beer.

Local Culture

The north of Thailand's culture is Lanna in origin and the people are very proud of their northern roots. The region is home to distinctly different food, music, arts, way of life and even language. Chiang Mai is also a melting pot of hill tribes and their own unique cultures.

Traditional lifestyle of the hilltribes

Tai Yai, Burmese in origin, harvest rice, farm, raise cattle and trade. Their craftsmanship lies in weaving, pottery, wood carving and bronzeware.

Akha have the largest population of any hill tribe in the region. Originating from Tibet and Southern China, they dwell on high grounds around 1,200 meters above sea-level. Within their villages they build a Spirit Gateway to protect them from evil spirits.

Lahu are also from Southern China and live in high areas. They are known as hunters and planters.

Karen live in various areas of the region which have valleys and riverbanks.

Hmong from southern China are located on high land. They raise livestock and grow rice, corn, tobacco and cabbage. They are also known for their embroidery and silver.

Tai Lue live in dwellings of usually only a single room wooden house built on high poles. They are skilled in weaving.

Lisu from southern China and Tibet are renowned for their colorful dress and also build their dwellings on high poles. They harvest rice and corn and their men are skilled in hunting.

Yao reside along mountain sides and grow corn and other crops. They are skilled blacksmiths, silversmiths and embroiders.

Events and Festivals

The roads along the moats of Chiang Mai are full of vehicles during the water splashing festival of Songkran

Bo Sang Umbrella Festival (งานเทศกาลร่มบ่อสร้าง) is held in January at Bo Sang Handicraft Centre. The festival features paper products, paper parasols in particular, cultural shows, a parade showing traditional ways of life, and several contests.

Flower Festival (งานมหกรรมไม้ดอกไม้ประดับ) is held in February. The festival includes ornamental garden flower contests, floral floats parade in the morning and beauty pageants. The parade begins at Chiang Mai Railway Station and passes Nawarat Bridge and ends at Nong Buak Hat Park.

Songkran Festival (งานประเพณีสงกรานต์) is held annually from 13 to 15 April. The 13th of April is the Great Songkran day featuring the revered Phra Phuttha Sihing (พระพุทธสิหิงค์) Buddha image parade around Chiang Mai town for bathing, sand pagoda forming, blessing of elders, and water splashing.

Doi Suthep Pilgrimage (งานประเพณีเดินขึ้นดอยสุเทพ) On the night of Visakha Bucha Day, worshippers gather to light candles and make the 7-kilometre pilgrimage up to the temple on Doi Suthep.

City Pillar Inthakin Festival (งานบูชาเสาอินทขิล) is held to invoke blessings of peace, happiness and prosperity for the city and its residents. Buddha images are paraded around the city. It is held at Wat Chedi Luang for 7 auspicious days and nights in the 7th lunar month.

Yi Peng Festival (งานประเพณียี่เป็ง) is held annually on Loy Krathong day (วันลอยกระทง). The festival features the release of lanterns into the sky to worship the gods. There are also fireworks, lantern contests, and beauty pageants.

Art

Chiang Mai province is known as one of the world's top centers for the cottage industry. The area is popular for traditional handicrafts made by craftsmen using skills which have been down through countless generations. They include: silverware, lacquerware, celadon pottery, silk and cotton, hand-painted paper umbrellas and more.

Local Food

- **Nam Prik Ong** is a type of chili paste which is made of minced pork and tomatoes. It is usually eaten with soft-boiled vegetables, pork crackling or deep-fried crunchy rice cakes.
- **Nam Prik Noom** meaning in English Chili Paste Young Man, is another kind of paste that is extremely popular in the north and eaten also by Thais of all regions. It is often eaten with pork crackling.
- **Sai Ua** is a local Chiang Mai sausage that is very aromatic and spicy and is usually eaten with sticky rice.
- **Kaeng** meaning curries are not made of coconut milk in the north.
  - Kaeng Hang-Le is northern-style pork curry
  - Kaeng Om is a spicy curry consisting of intestines
  - Kaeng Khae is a spicy curry consisting of vegetables.
- **Khanom Chin Nam Ngiao** is a traditional noodle dish with chicken of the North.
- **Khao Soi** is another popular noodle dish which can be made from chicken, pork or beef. What makes it unique is that it contains coconut milk and it is garnished with garlic.

Learn

Visitors to Chiang Mai have the opportunity to learn a variety of different Thai-style activities. These activities include Muay Thai (Thai Boxing), Thai cooking, Thai massage and Vipassana Meditation.

Retirement

There are approximately 5,000 expatriates living in Chiang Mai making it one of the most popular destinations for retirement in Thailand. This is probably due to the cool climate, natural surroundings and lower cost of living. .

Sports

There are two main sport stadiums in Mueang District, 700 Years stadium, and Province stadium. The 700 Years stadium is located on Klongchonpratan road, 7km from Chiang Mai University. There are swimming pool, diving pool, basketball stadium, main stadium, etc. There are 11 tennis courts (hard court).

Media/Contact

Nationwide Television, cable TV and local cable TV channels are available in Chiang Mai. Local and nationwide English newspapers and magazines are usually found in book stores.

Landline telephone system, high-speed internet (ADSL), all mobile phone systems, post offices, parcel services are available in Chiang Mai.

Sister cities

- Shanghai, China (2000)

- ▬ Yogyakarta, Indonesia (2007)
- ◉ Busan, South Korea (2009)
- ⊛ Pyongyang, North Korea (2009)
- ★ Hue, Vietnam (2009)
- ⚑ Phnom Penh, Cambodia (2009)

Gallery

View of the city of Chiang Mai from Doi Suthep

Bathing Elephants

Lahu farmers in the mountains of Amphoe Omkoi

Waroros Market, a market in downtown Chiang Mai

The river going through the town of Mae Chaem

Rice paddies in Chiang Mai province

Pine forests along road 108 in the mountains near Omkoi

Road 1099 eventually ends in the jungle at Mae Thun Noi, Amphoe Omkoi
Source (edited): "http://en.wikipedia.org/wiki/Chiang_Mai_Province"

Doi Inthanon

Doi Inthanon (Thai: ดอยอินทนนท์(Pronunciation)) is the highest mountain in Thailand. It is located in Mae Chaem District. The mountain was also known in the past as **Doi Luang** (meaning *big mountain*) or **Doi Ang Ka**, meaning *the crow's pond top*. Near the mountain's base was a pond where many crows gathered. The name *Doi Inthanon* was given in honour of the king Inthawichayanon, one of the last kings of Chiang Mai, who was concerned about the forests in the north and tried to preserve them. He ordered that after his death his remains shall be placed at Doi Luang, which was then renamed.

Geography

Doi Inthanon is part of a mountain range separating Burma from Thailand also known as **Loi Lar Mountain Range** or **Daen Lao Range**. This range, the westernmost of the Shan Highland system, separates the Salween watershed from the Mekong watershed. Other high peaks of the Loi Lar Mountain Range are Doi Luang Chiang Dao (2,175 m), Doi Pui (1,685 m), and Doi Suthep (1,601 m).

In 1954 the forests around Doi Inthanon were preserved as one of the original 14 National parks of Thailand. In 1972 and 1975 its area was increased, so it now covers 482.40 km². The park spreads from the lowlands at 800 m altitude up to the peak in 2565 m, thus covering many climatic and ecological different parts, thus with a total of 362 it has the second highest number of bird species of any national park in Thailand. The park is often called *The roof of Thailand*.

On the lower slope of Doi Inthanon, near the Karen hill tribe village Ban Sop Had, are the Wachirathan waterfalls (Thai: น้ำตกวชิรธาร), where the Wachirathan (lit. "Diamond Creek") tumbles over a granite escarpment.

Napamaytanidol Chedi

On the main road to the summit of Doi Inthanon stand the two Napamaytanidol Chedi. These temples were built to honor the 60th birthday of the King and Queen in 1987 and 1992 respectively.

Geology

Geologically the mountain is a granite batholith in a north-south oriented mountain range. The second-highest peak of this range is Doi Hua Mod Luang at 2,340 m.

Source (edited): "http://en.wikipedia.org/wiki/Doi_Inthanon"

Doi Suthep

Panoramic view of Doi Suthep as seen from Chiang Mai

Doi Suthep (ดอยสุเทพ), is a mountain located in Chiang Mai Province, Thailand.

Description

View of Chiang Mai from Doi Suthep

Doi Suthep (1,676 m) is one of the twin peaks of a granite mountain located west of Chiang Mai, the other peak is known as **Doi Pui** and is slightly taller (1,685 m).

Road in Doi Suthep - Doi Pui National Park

Doi Suthep is located 15 km away from Chiang Mai city centre. Most of the bedrock of the mountain is granite. The vegetation below c. 1,000 m is mostly deciduous forest and evergreen above this height.

The Doi Suthep - Doi Pui hill is part of a mountain chain separating Burma from Thailand also known as **Loi Lar Mountain Range** or **Daen Lao Range**. This range, the westernmost of the Shan Highland system, separates the Salween watershed from the Mekong watershed. Other high peaks of the Loi Lar Mountain Range are Doi Luang Chiang Dao (2,175 m), Doi Pui (1,685 m), and Doi Inthanon, the highest point in Thailand, reaching 2,565 m.

There are spectacular views of Chiang Mai city and its surroundings from the top of this mountain. Hmong tribal villages are located on the mountain sides.

The **Wat Phrathat Doi Suthep** temple is on top of the hill. This Buddhist place of worship dates back to the year 1383 when the first chedi was built. It is an important pilgrimage spot for the devout and a legend featuring a white elephant is connecteed to this revered site.

This mountain is part of the Doi Suthep - Doi Pui National Park. The park was established in 1981 and has an area of 261 km that includes the Wat Phrathat Doi Suthep temple as well as Bhubing palace, placed among flower gardens.

Doi Pui, the other peak of the massif, is located close by along a surfaced road as well as through forest paths. Hmong hill tribe people live in the surrounding area.

Source (edited): "http://en.wikipedia.org/wiki/Doi_Suthep"

Mae Taeng River

The **Mae Taeng River** (Thai: แม่น้ำแตง, RTGS: *Maenam Taeng*, Thai pronunciation: [mɛ̂ːnáːm tɛːŋ]) is a tributary of the Chao Phraya River. It originates in North Thailand near the border of Burma and flows through the mountainous region of the Chiang Mai Province. It is a popular river for white water rafting due to the existence of lots of average grade rapids.

Source (edited): "http://en.wikipedia.org/wiki/Mae_Taeng_River"

Ping River

The **Ping River** (Thai: แม่น้ำปิง, RTGS: *Maenam Ping*, IPA: [mɛ̂ːnáːm piŋ]), along with the Nan River, is one of the two main contributaries of Chao Phraya River. It originates at Doi Chiang Dao in Chiang Dao district, Chiang Mai Province. After passing Chiang Mai town, it flows though the provinces Lamphun, Tak, and Kamphaeng Phet. At the confluence with the Nan River at Nakhon Sawan (also named *Paknam Pho* in Thai) it forms the Chao Phraya River.

Tributaries

The principal tributary of the Ping is the Wang River.

Ping Basin

The Ping Basin is one of the largest drainage basins of the Chao Phraya Watershed, draining 33,896 km² of land area.

Greater Ping Basin

The greater Ping Basin, i.e. the basin of the entire Ping river system including its tributary the Wang River drains a total of 44,688 km² of land area.

National Parks

The Ping River flows through the Mae Ping National Park.

Source (edited): "http://en.wikipedia.org/wiki/Ping_River"

Queen Sirikit Botanic Garden

Queen Sirikit Botanic Garden

The Queen Sirikit Botanical Garden in Amphoe Mae Rim, Chiang Mai Province, Thailand was opened in 1992 and is maintained under the auspices of the Thai Ministry of Natural Resources and Environment. The facility's purpose is to conduct and promote botanical research, biodiversity and to conserve Thailand's natural plant resources. Originally named the Mae Sa Botanic Garden, it was renamed after Sirikit, Queen of Thailand in 1994.

Source (edited): "http://en.wikipedia.org/wiki/Queen_Sirikit_Botanic_Garden"

Ban Aen

Ban Aen (Thai: บ้านแอ่น) is a village and *tambon* (subdistrict) of Doi Tao District, in Chiang Mai Province, Thailand. In 2005 it had a total population of 2804 people. The *tambon* contains 4 villages.

There is a dam and reservoir in the vicinity.

Source (edited): "http://en.wikipedia.org/wiki/Ban_Aen"

Ban Chan, Galyani Vadhana

Ban Chan (Thai: บ้านชัย) is a *tambon* (subdistrict) of Galyani Vadhana District, in Chiang Mai Province, Thailand. In 2008 it had a total population of 3,707 people. The *tambon* contains 9 villages.

Source (edited): "http://en.wikipedia.org/wiki/Ban_Chan,_Galyani_Vadhana"

Ban Chang, Mae Taeng

Ban Chang (Thai: บ้านฉาง) is a *tambon* (subdistrict) of Mae Taeng District, in Chiang Mai Province, Thailand. In 2005 it had a total population of 5,488 people. The *tambon* contains 5 villages.

Source (edited): "http://en.wikipedia.org/wiki/Ban_Chang,_Mae_Taeng"

Ban Kat, Mae Wang

Ban Kat (Thai: บ้านกาด) is a *tambon* (subdistrict) of Mae Wang District, in Chiang Mai Province, Thailand. In 2005 it had a total population of 5,554 people. The *tambon* contains 13 villages.

Source (edited): "http://en.wikipedia.org/wiki/Ban_Kat,_Mae_Wang"

Ban Klang, San Pa Tong

Ban Klang (Thai: บ้านกลาง) is a *tambon* (subdistrict) of San Pa Tong District, in Chiang Mai Province, Thailand. In 2005 it had a total population of 9,969 people. The *tambon* contains 11 villages.

Source (edited): "http://en.wikipedia.org/wiki/Ban_Klang,_San_Pa_Tong"

Ban Luang, Chom Thong

Ban Luang (Thai: บ้านหลวง) is a *tambon* (subdistrict) of Chom Thong District, in Chiang Mai Province, Thailand. In 2005 it had a total population of 15,618 people. The *tambon* contains 23 villages.

Source (edited): "http://en.wikipedia.org/wiki/Ban_Luang,_Chom_Thong"

Ban Luang, Mae Ai

Ban Luang (Thai: บ้านหลวง) is a *tambon* (subdistrict) of Mae Ai District, in Chiang Mai Province, Thailand. In 2005 it had a total population of 7,346 people. The *tambon* contains 10 villages. Source (edited): "http://en.wikipedia.org/wiki/Ban_Luang,_Mae_Ai"

Ban Mae

Ban Mae (Thai: บ้านแม) is a *tambon* (subdistrict) of San Pa Tong District, in Chiang Mai Province, Thailand. In 2005 it had a total population of 6,872 people. The *tambon* contains 14 villages. Source (edited): "http://en.wikipedia.org/wiki/Ban_Mae"

Ban Pae

Ban Pae (Thai: บ้านแปะ) is a *tambon* (subdistrict) of Chom Thong District, in Chiang Mai Province, Thailand. In 2005 it had a total population of 12,050 people. The *tambon* contains 18 villages. Source (edited): "http://en.wikipedia.org/wiki/Ban_Pae"

Ban Pao, Mae Taeng

Ban Pao (Thai: บ้านเป้า) is a *tambon* (subdistrict) of Mae Taeng District, in Chiang Mai Province, Thailand. In 2005 it had a total population of 4,029 people. The *tambon* contains 7 villages. Source (edited): "http://en.wikipedia.org/wiki/Ban_Pao,_Mae_Taeng"

Ban Pong, Hang Dong

Ban Pong (Thai: บ้านปง) is a *tambon* (subdistrict) of Hang Dong District, in Chiang Mai Province, Thailand. In 2005 it had a total population of 4827 people. The *tambon* contains 11 villages. Source (edited): "http://en.wikipedia.org/wiki/Ban_Pong,_Hang_Dong"

Ban Pong, Phrao

Ban Pong (Thai: บ้านโป่ง) is a *tambon* (subdistrict) of Phrao District, in Chiang Mai Province, Thailand. In 2005 it had a total population of 4053 people. The *tambon* contains 8 villages. Source (edited): "http://en.wikipedia.org/wiki/Ban_Pong,_Phrao"

Ban Sahakon

Ban Sahakon (Thai: บ้านสหกรณ์) is a *tambon* (subdistrict) of Mae On District, in Chiang Mai Province, Thailand. In 2005 it had a total population of 3,043 people. The *tambon* contains 8 villages. Source (edited): "http://en.wikipedia.org/wiki/Ban_Sahakon"

Ban Tan, Hot

Ban Tan (Thai: บ้านตาล) is a *tambon* (subdistrict) of Hot District, in Chiang Mai Province, Thailand. In 2005 it had a total population of 5242 people. The *tambon* contains 10 villages. Source (edited): "http://en.wikipedia.org/wiki/Ban_Tan,_Hot"

Ban Thap

Ban Thap (Thai: บ้านทับ) is a *tambon* (subdistrict) of Mae Chaem District, in Chiang Mai Province, Thailand.In 2005 it had a total population of 6,234 people. The *tambon* contains 13 villages. Source (edited): "http://en.wikipedia.org/wiki/Ban_Thap"

Ban Waen

Ban Waen (Thai: บ้านแหวน) is a *tambon* (subdistrict) of Hang Dong District, in Chiang Mai Province, Thailand.In 2005 it had a total population of 9537 people. The *tambon* contains 13 villages. Source (edited): "http://en.wikipedia.org/wiki/Ban_Waen"

Bo Kaeo, Samoeng

Bo Kaeo (Thai: บ่อแก้ว) is a *tambon* (subdistrict) of Samoeng District, in Chiang Mai Province, Thailand.In 2005 it had a total population of 7,135 people. The *tambon* contains 10 villages. Source (edited): "http://en.wikipedia.org/wiki/Bo_Kaeo,_Samoeng"

Bo Luang

Bo Luang (Thai: บ่อหลวง) is a *tambon* (subdistrict) of Hot District, in Chiang Mai Province, Thailand.In 2005 it had a total population of 11,958 people. The *tambon* contains 12 villages. Source (edited): "http://en.wikipedia.org/wiki/Bo_Luang"

Bo Sali

Bo Sali (Thai: บ่อสลี) is a *tambon* (subdistrict) of Hot District, in Chiang Mai Province, Thailand.In 2005 it had a total population of 7,926 people. The *tambon* contains 10 villages. Source (edited): "http://en.wikipedia.org/wiki/Bo_Sali"

Bong Tan

Bong Tan (Thai: บงตัน) is a *tambon* (subdistrict) of Doi Tao District, in Chiang Mai Province, Thailand.In 2005 it had a total population of 4678 people. The *tambon* contains 6 villages. Source (edited): "http://en.wikipedia.org/wiki/Bong_Tan"

Buak Khang

Buak Khang (Thai: บวกค้าง) is a *tambon* (subdistrict) of San Kamphaeng District, in Chiang Mai Province, Thailand.In 2005 it had a total population of 7,851 people. The *tambon* contains 13 villages. Source (edited): "http://en.wikipedia.org/wiki/Buak_Khang"

Chae Chang

Chae Chang (Thai: แช่ช้าง) is a *tambon* (subdistrict) of San Kamphaeng District, in Chiang Mai Province, Thailand.In 2005 it had a total population of 7,585 people. The *tambon* contains 9 villages. Source (edited): "http://en.wikipedia.org/wiki/Chae_Chang"

Chaem Luang

Chaem Luang (Thai: แจ่มหลวง) is a *tambon* (subdistrict) of Galyani Vadhana District, in Chiang Mai Province, Thailand. In 2008 it had a total population of 3,527 people. The *tambon* contains 7 villages.

Source (edited): "http://en.wikipedia.org/wiki/Chaem_Luang"

Chai Sathan

Chai Sathan (Thai: ไชยสถาน) is a *tambon* (subdistrict) of Saraphi District, in Chiang Mai Province, Thailand. In 2005 it had a total population of 4567 people. The *tambon* contains 8 villages.

Source (edited): "http://en.wikipedia.org/wiki/Chai_Sathan"

Chang Khlan

Chang Khlan (Thai: ช้างคลาน) is a *tambon* (subdistrict) of Mueang Chiang Mai District, in Chiang Mai Province, Thailand. In 2005 it had a total population of 15,368 people.

Source (edited): "http://en.wikipedia.org/wiki/Chang_Khlan"

Chang Khoeng

Chang Khoeng (Thai: ช่างเคิ่ง) is a *tambon* (subdistrict) of Mae Chaem District, in Chiang Mai Province, Thailand. In 2005 it had a total population of 11,206 people. The *tambon* contains 19 villages.

Source (edited): "http://en.wikipedia.org/wiki/Chang_Khoeng"

Chang Moi

Chang Moi (Thai: ช้างม่อย) is a *tambon* (subdistrict) of Mueang Chiang Mai District, in Chiang Mai Province, Thailand. In 2005 it had a total population of 9,528 people.

Source (edited): "http://en.wikipedia.org/wiki/Chang_Moi"

Chang Phueak, Mueang Chiang Mai

Chang Phueak (Thai: ช้างเผือก) is a *tambon* (subdistrict) of Mueang Chiang Mai District, in Chiang Mai Province, Thailand. In 2005 it had a total population of 27,421 people. The *tambon* contains 5 villages.

Source (edited): "http://en.wikipedia.org/wiki/Chang_Phueak,_Mueang_Chiang_Mai"

Chiang Dao

Chiang Dao (Thai: เชียงดาว) is a town and *tambon* (subdistrict) of Chiang Dao District, in Chiang Mai Province, Thailand. In 2005 it had a total population of 15,194 people. The *tambon* contains 16 villages.

Source (edited): "http://en.wikipedia.org/wiki/Chiang_Dao"

Cho Lae

Cho Lae (Thai: ช่อแล) is a *tambon* (subdistrict) of Mae Taeng District, in Chiang Mai Province, Thailand. In 2005 it had a total population of 4,787 people. The *tambon* contains 16 villages.

Source (edited): "http://en.wikipedia.org/wiki/Cho_Lae"

Choeng Doi

Choeng Doi (Thai: เชิงดอย) is a *tambon* (subdistrict) of Doi Saket District, in Chiang Mai Province, Thailand.In 2005 it had a total population of 10,750 people. The *tambon* contains 13 villages. Source (edited): "http://en.wikipedia.org/wiki/Choeng_Doi"

Chom Phu

Chom Phu (Thai: ชมภู) is a *tambon* (subdistrict) of Saraphi District, in Chiang Mai Province, Thailand.In 2005 it had a total population of 6,873 people. The *tambon* contains 8 villages. Source (edited): "http://en.wikipedia.org/wiki/Chom_Phu"

Doi Kaeo

Doi Kaeo (Thai: ดอยแก้ว) is a *tambon* (subdistrict) of Chom Thong District, in Chiang Mai Province, Thailand.In 2005 it had a total population of 5,128 people. The *tambon* contains 9 villages. Source (edited): "http://en.wikipedia.org/wiki/Doi_Kaeo"

Doi Lo

Doi Lo (Thai: ดอยหล่อ) is a *tambon* (subdistrict) of Doi Lo District, in Chiang Mai Province, Thailand.In 2005 it had a total population of 12,809 people. The *tambon* contains 26 villages. Source (edited): "http://en.wikipedia.org/wiki/Doi_Lo"

Doi Tao

Doi Tao (Thai: ดอยเต่า) is a *tambon* (subdistrict) of Doi Tao District, in Chiang Mai Province, Thailand.In 2005 it had a total population of 6,790 people. The *tambon* contains 10 villages. Source (edited): "http://en.wikipedia.org/wiki/Doi_Tao"

Don Kaeo, Mae Rim

Don Kaeo (Thai: ดอนแก้ว) is a *tambon* (subdistrict) of Mae Rim District, in Chiang Mai Province, Thailand.In 2005 it had a total population of 14,286 people. The *tambon* contains 10 villages. Source (edited): "http://en.wikipedia.org/wiki/Don_Kaeo,_Mae_Rim"

Don Kaeo, Saraphi

Don Kaeo (Thai: ดอนแก้ว) is a *tambon* (subdistrict) of Saraphi District, in Chiang Mai Province, Thailand.In 2005 it had a total population of 3,913 people. The *tambon* contains 7 villages. Source (edited): "http://en.wikipedia.org/wiki/Don_Kaeo,_Saraphi"

Don Pao

Don Pao (Thai: ดอนเปา) is a *tambon* (subdistrict) of Mae Wang District, in Chiang Mai Province, Thailand.In 2005 it had a total population of 7,196 people. The *tambon* contains 10 villages. Source (edited): "http://en.wikipedia.org/wiki/Don_Pao"

Fa Ham

Fa Ham (Thai: ฟ้าฮ่าม) is a *tambon* (subdistrict) of Mueang Chiang Mai District, in Chiang Mai Province, Thailand. In 2005 it had a total population of 7,193 people. The *tambon* contains 7 villages.

Source (edited): "http://en.wikipedia.org/wiki/Fa_Ham"

Haiya

Haiya (Thai: หายยา) is a *tambon* (subdistrict) of Mueang Chiang Mai District, in Chiang Mai Province, Thailand. In 2005 it had a total population of 14,818 people.

Source (edited): "http://en.wikipedia.org/wiki/Haiya"

Han Kaeo

Han Kaeo (Thai: หารแก้ว) is a *tambon* (subdistrict) of Hang Dong District, in Chiang Mai Province, Thailand. In 2005 it had a total population of 5767 people. The *tambon* contains 9 villages.

Source (edited): "http://en.wikipedia.org/wiki/Han_Kaeo"

Hang Dong, Hang Dong

Hang Dong (Thai: หางดง) is a *tambon* (subdistrict) of Hang Dong District, in Chiang Mai Province, Thailand. In 2005 it had a total population of 2531 people. The *tambon* contains 13 villages.

Source (edited): "http://en.wikipedia.org/wiki/Hang_Dong,_Hang_Dong"

Hang Dong, Hot

Hang Dong (Thai: หางดง) is a *tambon* (subdistrict) of Hot District, in Chiang Mai Province, Thailand. In 2005 it had a total population of 15,303 people. The *tambon* contains 13 villages.

Source (edited): "http://en.wikipedia.org/wiki/Hang_Dong,_Hot"

Hot, Hot

Hot (Thai: ฮอด) is a *tambon* (subdistrict) of Hot District, in Chiang Mai Province, Thailand. In 2005 it had a total population of 3,313 people. The *tambon* contains 6 villages.

Source (edited): "http://en.wikipedia.org/wiki/Hot,_Hot"

Huai Kaeo, Mae On

Huai Kaeo (Thai: ห้วยแก้ว) is a *tambon* (subdistrict) of Mae On District, in Chiang Mai Province, Thailand. In 2005 it had a total population of 2,888 people. The *tambon* contains 8 villages.

Source (edited): "http://en.wikipedia.org/wiki/Huai_Kaeo,_Mae_On"

Huai Sai, Mae Rim

Huai Sai (Thai: ห้วยทราย) is a *tambon* (subdistrict) of Mae Rim District, in Chiang Mai Province, Thailand. In 2005 it had a total population of 4,253 people. The *tambon* contains 5 villages.

Source (edited): "http://en.wikipedia.org/wiki/Huai_Sai,_Mae_Rim"

Huai Sai, San Kamphaeng

Huai Sai (Thai: ห้วยทราย) is a *tambon* (subdistrict) of San Kamphaeng District, in Chiang Mai Province, Thailand.In 2005 it had a total population of 6,217 people. The *tambon* contains 8 villages.

Source (edited): "http://en.wikipedia.org/wiki/Huai_Sai,_San_Kamphaeng"

Inthakhin

Ox-cart, Inthakhin

Inthakhin (Thai: อินทขิล) is a *tambon* (subdistrict) of Mae Taeng District, in Chiang Mai Province, Thailand.In 2005 it had a total population of 14,097 people. The *tambon* contains 18 villages.

Source (edited): "http://en.wikipedia.org/wiki/Inthakhin"

Khilek, Mae Rim

Khilek (Thai: ขี้เหล็ก) is a *tambon* (subdistrict) of Mae Rim District, in Chiang Mai Province, Thailand.In 2005 it had a total population of 7,357 people. The *tambon* contains 10 villages.

Source (edited): "http://en.wikipedia.org/wiki/Khilek,_Mae_Rim"

Khilek, Mae Taeng

Khilek (Thai: ขี้เหล็ก) is a *tambon* (subdistrict) of Mae Taeng District, in Chiang Mai Province, Thailand.In 2005 it had a total population of 9,609 people. The *tambon* contains 10 villages.

Source (edited): "http://en.wikipedia.org/wiki/Khilek,_Mae_Taeng"

Khua Mung

Khua Mung (Thai: ข่วมุง) is a *tambon* (subdistrict) of Saraphi District, in Chiang Mai Province, Thailand.In 2005 it had a total population of 5,510 people. The *tambon* contains 10 villages.

Source (edited): "http://en.wikipedia.org/wiki/Khua_Mung"

Khuang Pao

Khuang Pao (Thai: ข่วงเปา) is a *tambon* (subdistrict) of Chom Thong District, in Chiang Mai Province, Thailand.In 2005 it had a total population of 10,912 people. The *tambon* contains 12 villages.

Source (edited): "http://en.wikipedia.org/wiki/Khuang_Pao"

Khuean Phak

Khuean Phak (Thai: เขื่อนผาก) is a *tambon* (subdistrict) of Phrao District, in Chiang Mai Province, Thailand.In 2005 it had a total population of 5,021 people. The *tambon* contains 10 villages.

Source (edited): "http://en.wikipedia.org/wiki/Khuean_Phak"

Khun Khong

Khun Khong (Thai: ขุนคง) is a *tambon* (subdistrict) of Hang Dong District, in Chiang Mai Province, Thailand. In 2005 it had a total population of 4772 people. The *tambon* contains 9 villages. Source (edited): "http://en.wikipedia.org/wiki/Khun_Khong"

Kong Khaek

Kong Khaek (Thai: กองแขก) is a *tambon* (subdistrict) of Mae Chaem District, in Chiang Mai Province, Thailand. In 2005 it had a total population of 6,205 people. The *tambon* contains 12 villages. Source (edited): "http://en.wikipedia.org/wiki/Kong_Khaek"

Kuet Chang

Kuet Chang (Thai: กึ๊ดช้าง) is a *tambon* (subdistrict) of Mae Taeng District, in Chiang Mai Province, Thailand. In 2005 it had a total population of 5,834 people. The *tambon* contains 8 villages. Source (edited): "http://en.wikipedia.org/wiki/Kuet_Chang"

Long Khot

Long Khot (Thai: โหล่งขอด) is a *tambon* (subdistrict) of Phrao District, in Chiang Mai Province, Thailand. In 2005 it had a total population of 5,032 people. The *tambon* contains 9 villages. Source (edited): "http://en.wikipedia.org/wiki/Long_Khot"

Luang Nuea

Luang Nuea (Thai: ลวงเหนือ) is a *tambon* (subdistrict) of Doi Saket District, in Chiang Mai Province, Thailand. In 2005 it had a total population of 6,330 people. The *tambon* contains 10 villages. Source (edited): "http://en.wikipedia.org/wiki/Luang_Nuea"

Mae Ai

Mae Ai (Thai: ?) is a town and *tambon* (subdistrict) of Mae Ai District, in Chiang Mai Province, Thailand. In 2005 it had a total population of 9,987 people. The *tambon* contains 22 villages. Source (edited): "http://en.wikipedia.org/wiki/Mae_Ai"

Mae Daet

Mae Daet (Thai: แม่แดด) is a *tambon* (subdistrict) of Galyani Vadhana District, in Chiang Mai Province, Thailand. In 2008 it had a total population of 3,359 people. The *tambon* contains 7 villages. Source (edited): "http://en.wikipedia.org/wiki/Mae_Daet"

Mae Faek

Mae Faek (Thai: แม่แฝก) is a *tambon* (subdistrict) of San Sai District, in Chiang Mai Province, Thailand. In 2005 it had a total population of 9,619 people. The *tambon* contains 12 villages. Source (edited): "http://en.wikipedia.org/wiki/Mae_Faek"

Mae Faek Mai

Mae Faek Mai (Thai: แม่แฝกใหม่) is a *tambon* (subdistrict) of San Sai District, in Chiang Mai Province, Thailand. In 2005 it had a total population of 7,575 people. The *tambon* contains 12 villages.

Source (edited): "http://en.wikipedia.org/wiki/Mae_Faek_Mai"

Mae Hia

Mae Hia (Thai: ตำบลแม่เหียะ) is a *tambon* (subdistrict) of Mueang Chiang Mai District, in Chiang Mai Province, Thailand. In 2005 it had a total population of 15,656 people. The *tambon* contains 10 villages.

Source (edited): "http://en.wikipedia.org/wiki/Mae_Hia"

Mae Ho Phra

Mae Ho Phra (Thai: แม่หอพระ) is a *tambon* (subdistrict) of Mae Taeng District, in Chiang Mai Province, Thailand. In 2005 it had a total population of 5,643 people. The *tambon* contains 9 villages.

Source (edited): "http://en.wikipedia.org/wiki/Mae_Ho_Phra"

Mae Hoi Ngoen

Mae Hoi Ngoen (Thai: แม่ฮ้อยเงิน) is a *tambon* (subdistrict) of Doi Saket District, in Chiang Mai Province, Thailand. In 2005 it had a total population of 3,848 people. The *tambon* contains 6 villages.

Source (edited): "http://en.wikipedia.org/wiki/Mae_Hoi_Ngoen"

Mae Ka

Mae Ka (Thai: แม่ก๊า) is a *tambon* (subdistrict) of San Pa Tong District, in Chiang Mai Province, Thailand. In 2005 it had a total population of 7,630 people. The *tambon* contains 14 villages.

Source (edited): "http://en.wikipedia.org/wiki/Mae_Ka"

Mae Ka, Fang

Mae Ka (Thai: แม่คะ) is a *tambon* (subdistrict) of Fang District, in Chiang Mai Province, Thailand. In 2005 it had a total population of 14,542 people. The *tambon* contains 15 villages.

Source (edited): "http://en.wikipedia.org/wiki/Mae_Ka,_Fang"

Mae Khue

Mae Khue (Thai: แม่คือ) is a *tambon* (subdistrict) of Doi Saket District, in Chiang Mai Province, Thailand. In 2005 it had a total population of 4,797 people. The *tambon* contains 6 villages.

Source (edited): "http://en.wikipedia.org/wiki/Mae_Khue"

Mae Na

Mae Na (Thai: แม่นะ) is a *tambon* (subdistrict) of Chiang Dao District, in Chiang Mai Province, Thailand. In 2005 it had a total population of 9,782 people. The *tambon* contains 13 villages.

Source (edited): "http://en.wikipedia.org/wiki/Mae_Na"

Mae Na Chon

Mae Na Chon (Thai: ?) is a *tambon* (subdistrict) of Mae Chaem District, in Chiang Mai Province, Thailand.In 2005 it had a total population of 10,184 people. The *tambon* contains 19 villages. Source (edited): "http://en.wikipedia.org/wiki/Mae_Na_Chon"

Mae Na Wang

Mae Na Wang (Thai: ?) is a *tambon* (subdistrict) of Mae Ai District, in Chiang Mai Province, Thailand.In 2005 it had a total population of 14,320 people. The *tambon* contains 14 villages. Source (edited): "http://en.wikipedia.org/wiki/Mae_Na_Wang"

Mae Ngon

Mae Ngon (Thai: แม่งอน) is a *tambon* (subdistrict) of Fang District, in Chiang Mai Province, Thailand. In 2005 it had a total population of 17,715 people. The *tambon* contains 18 villages. Source (edited): "http://en.wikipedia.org/wiki/Mae_Ngon"

Mae Pang

Mae Pang (Thai: ?) is a *tambon* (subdistrict) of Phrao District, in Chiang Mai Province, Thailand.In 2005 it had a total population of 6,571 people. The *tambon* contains 13 villages. Source (edited): "http://en.wikipedia.org/wiki/Mae_Pang"

Mae Pong

Mae Pong (Thai: แม่โป่ง) is a *tambon* (subdistrict) of Doi Saket District, in Chiang Mai Province, Thailand.In 2005 it had a total population of 5,589 people. The *tambon* contains 10 villages. Source (edited): "http://en.wikipedia.org/wiki/Mae_Pong"

Mae Pu Kha

Mae Pu Kha (Thai: แม่ปูคา) is a *tambon* (subdistrict) of San Kamphaeng District, in Chiang Mai Province, Thailand.In 2005 it had a total population of 5,969 people. The *tambon* contains 9 villages. Source (edited): "http://en.wikipedia.org/wiki/Mae_Pu_Kha"

Mae Raem

Orchids growing at the Mae Ram Orchid and Butterfly Farm, Mae Raem

Mae Raem (Thai: แม่แรม) is a *tambon* (subdistrict) of Mae Rim District, in Chiang Mai Province, Thailand. In 2005 it had a total population of 8,264 people. The *tambon* contains 12 villages.
Source (edited): "http://en.wikipedia.org/wiki/Mae_Raem"

Mae Sa

Mae Sa (Thai: ?) is a *tambon* (subdistrict) of Mae Rim District, in Chiang Mai Province, Thailand. In 2005 it had a total population of 6,448 people. The *tambon* contains 6 villages.
Source (edited): "http://en.wikipedia.org/wiki/Mae_Sa"

Mae Sao

Mae Sao (Thai: ?) is a *tambon* (subdistrict) of Mae Ai District, in Chiang Mai Province, Thailand. In 2005 it had a total population of 12,789 people. The *tambon* contains 20 villages.
Source (edited): "http://en.wikipedia.org/wiki/Mae_Sao"

Mae Sap

Mae Sap (Thai: แม่สาบ) is a *tambon* (subdistrict) of Samoeng District, in Chiang Mai Province, Thailand. In 2005 it had a total population of 3,464 people. The *tambon* contains 10 villages.
Source (edited): "http://en.wikipedia.org/wiki/Mae_Sap"

Mae Soi

Mae Soi (Thai: แม่สอย) is a *tambon* (subdistrict) of Chom Thong District, in Chiang Mai Province, Thailand. In 2005 it had a total population of 8,715 people. The *tambon* contains 14 villages.
Source (edited): "http://en.wikipedia.org/wiki/Mae_Soi"

Mae Suek

Mae Suek (Thai: ?) is a *tambon* (subdistrict) of Mae Chaem District, in Chiang Mai Province, Thailand. In 2005 it had a total population of 11,577 people. The *tambon* contains 11 villages.
Source (edited): "http://en.wikipedia.org/wiki/Mae_Suek"

Mae Sun

Mae Sun (Thai: แม่สูน) is a *tambon* (subdistrict) of Fang District, in Chiang Mai Province, Thailand. In 2005 it had a total population of 15,019 people. The *tambon* contains 17 villages.
Source (edited): "http://en.wikipedia.

Mae Taeng

Mae Taeng (Thai: แม่แตง) is a town and *tambon* (subdistrict) of Mae Taeng District, in Chiang Mai Province, Thailand.In 2005 it had a total population of 4,548 people. The *tambon* contains 8 villages.

Source (edited): "http://en.wikipedia.org/wiki/Mae_Taeng"

Mae Tha

Mae Tha (Thai: ?) is a *tambon* (subdistrict) of Mae On District, in Chiang Mai Province, Thailand.In 2005 it had a total population of 4,812 people. The *tambon* contains 7 villages.

Source (edited): "http://en.wikipedia.org/wiki/Mae_Tha"

Mae Thalop

Mae Thalop (Thai: แม่ทะลบ) is a *tambon* (subdistrict) of Chai Prakan District, in Chiang Mai Province, Thailand.In 2005 it had a total population of 7,415 people. The *tambon* contains 6 villages.

Source (edited): "http://en.wikipedia.org/wiki/Mae_Thalop"

Mae Tuen

Mae Tuen (Thai: negro paradise) is a *tambon* (subdistrict) of Omkoi District, in Chiang Mai Province, Thailand.In 2005 it had a total population of 9,180 people. The *tambon* contains 16 villages.

Source (edited): "http://en.wikipedia.org/wiki/Mae_Tuen"

Mae Waen

Mae Waen (Thai: ?) is a *tambon* (subdistrict) of Phrao District, in Chiang Mai Province, Thailand.In 2005 it had a total population of 5,517 people. The *tambon* contains 11 villages.

Source (edited): "http://en.wikipedia.org/wiki/Mae_Waen"

Mae Win

Mae Win (Thai: แม่วิน) is a *tambon* (subdistrict) of Mae Wang District, in Chiang Mai Province, Thailand.In 2005 it had a total population of 10,879 people. The *tambon* contains 19 villages.

Source (edited): "http://en.wikipedia.org/wiki/Mae_Win"

Makham Luang

Makham Luang (Thai: มะขามหลวง) is a *tambon* (subdistrict) of San Pa Tong District, in Chiang Mai Province, Thailand.In 2005 it had a total population of 6,575 people. The *tambon* contains 11 villages.

Source (edited): "http://en.wikipedia.org/wiki/Makham_Luang"

Makhun Wan

Makhun Wan (Thai: มะขุนหวาน) is a *tambon* (subdistrict) of San Pa Tong District, in Chiang Mai Province, Thailand.In 2005 it had a total population of 5,399 people. The *tambon* contains 7 villages.

Source (edited): "http://en.wikipedia.org/wiki/Makhun_Wan"

Malika, Thailand

Malika (Thai: ตำบลมะลิกา) is a *tambon* (subdistrict) of Mae Ai District, in Chiang Mai Province, Thailand.In 2005 it had a total population of 4,510 people. The *tambon* contains 11 villages.
Source (edited): "http://en.wikipedia.org/wiki/Malika,_Thailand"

Mon Chong

Mon Chong (Thai: ?) is a *tambon* (subdistrict) of Omkoi District, in Chiang Mai Province, Thailand.In 2005 it had a total population of 6,008 people. The *tambon* contains 9 villages.
Source (edited): "http://en.wikipedia.org/wiki/Mon_Chong"

Mon Pin

Mon Pin (Thai: ม่อนปิ่น) is a *tambon* (subdistrict) of Fang District, in Chiang Mai Province, Thailand.In 2005 it had a total population of 19,123 people. The *tambon* contains 22 villages.
Source (edited): "http://en.wikipedia.org/wiki/Mon_Pin"

Mueang Haeng

Mueang Haeng (Thai: ?) is a *tambon* (subdistrict) of Wiang Haeng District, in Chiang Mai Province, Thailand.In 2005 it had a total population of 8,631 people. The *tambon* contains 12 villages.
Source (edited): "http://en.wikipedia.org/wiki/Mueang_Haeng"

Mueang Kaeo

Mueang Kaeo (Thai: ?) is a *tambon* (subdistrict) of Mae Rim District, in Chiang Mai Province, Thailand.In 2005 it had a total population of 5423 people. The *tambon* contains 9 villages.
Source (edited): "http://en.wikipedia.org/wiki/Mueang_Kaeo"

Mueang Kai

Mueang Kai (Thai: เมืองก๋าย) is a *tambon* (subdistrict) of Mae Taeng District, in Chiang Mai Province, Thailand.In 2005 it had a total population of 1,938 people. The *tambon* contains 5 villages.
Source (edited): "http://en.wikipedia.org/wiki/Mueang_Kai"

Mueang Khong

Mueang Khong (Thai: เชียงของเมืองคอง) is a *tambon* (subdistrict) of Chiang Dao District, in Chiang Mai Province, Thailand.In 2005 it had a total population of 4,244 people. The *tambon* contains 6 villages.
Source (edited): "http://en.wikipedia.org/wiki/Mueang_Khong"

Mueang Len

Mueang Len (Thai: เมืองเล็น) is a *tambon* (subdistrict) of San Sai District, in Chiang Mai Province, Thailand.In 2005 it had a total population of 2,535 people. The *tambon* contains 5 villages.
Source (edited): "http://en.wikipedia.org/wiki/Mueang_Len"

Mueang Na

Mueang Na (Thai: เมืองนะ) is a *tambon* (subdistrict) of Chiang Dao District, in Chiang Mai Province, Thailand.In 2005 it had a total population of 31,574 people. The *tambon* contains 14 villages. Source (edited): "http://en.wikipedia.org/wiki/Mueang_Na"

Mueang Ngai

Mueang Ngai (Thai: เมืองงาย) is a *tambon* (subdistrict) of Chiang Dao District, in Chiang Mai Province, Thailand.In 2005 it had a total population of 6,513 people. The *tambon* contains 11 villages. Source (edited): "http://en.wikipedia.org/wiki/Mueang_Ngai"

Muet Ka

Muet Ka (Thai: มืดกา) is a *tambon* (subdistrict) of Doi Tao District, in Chiang Mai Province, Thailand.In 2005 it had a total population of 3363 people. The *tambon* contains 5 villages. Source (edited): "http://en.wikipedia.org/wiki/Muet_Ka"

Na Kho Ruea

Na Kho Ruea (Thai: นาคอเรือ) is a *tambon* (subdistrict) of Hot District, in Chiang Mai Province, Thailand.In 2005 it had a total population of 4551 people. The *tambon* contains 10 villages. Source (edited): "http://en.wikipedia.org/wiki/Na_Kho_Ruea"

Na Kian

Na Kian (Thai: นาเกียน) is a *tambon* (subdistrict) of Omkoi District, in Chiang Mai Province, Thailand.In 2005 it had a total population of 7,897 people. The *tambon* contains 21 villages. Source (edited): "http://en.wikipedia.org/wiki/Na_Kian"

Nam Bo Luang

Nam Bo Luang (Thai: น้ำบ่อหลวง) is a *tambon* (subdistrict) of San Pa Tong District, in Chiang Mai Province, Thailand.In 2005 it had a total population of 4,917 people. The *tambon* contains 11 villages. Source (edited): "http://en.wikipedia.org/wiki/Nam_Bo_Luang"

Nam Phrae, Hang Dong

Nam Phrae (Thai: น้ำแพร่) is a *tambon* (subdistrict) of Hang Dong District, in Chiang Mai Province, Thailand.In 2005 it had a total population of 6031 people. The *tambon* contains 11 villages. Source (edited): "http://en.wikipedia.org/wiki/Nam_Phrae,_Hang_Dong"

Nam Phrae, Phrao

Nam Phrae (Thai: น้ำแพร่) is a *tambon* (subdistrict) of Phrao District, in Chiang Mai Province, Thailand.In 2005 it had a total population of 3,484 people. The *tambon* contains 8 villages. Source (edited): "http://en.wikipedia.org/wiki/Nam_Phrae,_Phrao"

Nong Bua, Chai Prakan

Nong Bua (Thai: หนองบัว) is a *tambon* (subdistrict) of Chai Prakan District, in Chiang Mai Province, Thailand. In 2005 it had a total population of 16,374 people. The *tambon* contains 11 villages. Source (edited): "http://en.wikipedia.org/wiki/Nong_Bua,_Chai_Prakan"

Nong Chom

Nong Chom (Thai: หนองจ๊อม) is a *tambon* (subdistrict) of San Sai District, in Chiang Mai Province, Thailand. In 2005 it had a total population of 13,657 people. The *tambon* contains 9 villages. Source (edited): "http://en.wikipedia.org/wiki/Nong_Chom"

Nong Faek

Nong Faek (Thai: หนองแฝก) is a *tambon* (subdistrict) of Saraphi District, in Chiang Mai Province, Thailand. In 2005 it had a total population of 5271 people. The *tambon* contains 9 villages. Source (edited): "http://en.wikipedia.org/wiki/Nong_Faek"

Nong Han, San Sai

Nong Han (Thai: หนองหาร) is a *tambon* (subdistrict) of San Sai District, in Chiang Mai Province, Thailand. In 2005 it had a total population of 16,463 people. The *tambon* contains 13 villages. Source (edited): "http://en.wikipedia.org/wiki/Nong_Han,_San_Sai"

Nong Hoi

Nong Hoi (Thai: ?) is a *tambon* (subdistrict) of Mueang Chiang Mai District, in Chiang Mai Province, Thailand. In 2005 it had a total population of 13,144 people. The *tambon* contains 6 villages. Source (edited): "http://en.wikipedia.org/wiki/Nong_Hoi"

Nong Kaeo, Hang Dong

Nong Kaeo (Thai: หนองแก๋ว) is a *tambon* (subdistrict) of Hang Dong District, in Chiang Mai Province, Thailand. In 2005 it had a total population of 5276 people. The *tambon* contains 9 villages. Source (edited): "http://en.wikipedia.org/wiki/Nong_Kaeo,_Hang_Dong"

Nong Khwai

Nong Khwai (Thai: หนองควาย) is a *tambon* (subdistrict) of Hang Dong District, in Chiang Mai Province, Thailand. In 2005 it had a total population of 8344 people. The *tambon* contains 12 villages. Source (edited): "http://en.wikipedia.org/wiki/Nong_Khwai"

Nong Pa Khrang

Nong Pa Khrang (Thai: หนองป่าครั่ง "Forest Marsh of Lac") is a *tambon* (subdistrict) of Mueang Chiang Mai District, in Chiang Mai Province, Thailand. In 2005 it had a total population of 8,423 people. The *tambon* contains 7 mubans (villages). Source (edited): "http://en.wikipedia.org/wiki/Nong_Pa_Khrang"

Nong Phueng

Nong Phueng (Thai: หนองผึ้ง) is a *tambon* (subdistrict) of Saraphi District, in Chiang Mai Province, Thailand. In 2005 it had a total population of 11,429 people. The *tambon* contains 8 villages. Source (edited): "http://en.wikipedia.org/wiki/Nong_Phueng"

Nong Tong

Nong Tong (Thai: หนองตอง) is a *tambon* (subdistrict) of Hang Dong District, in Chiang Mai Province, Thailand. In 2005 it had a total population of 9,512 people. The *tambon* contains 14 villages. Source (edited): "http://en.wikipedia.org/wiki/Nong_Tong"

Nong Yaeng

Nong Yaeng (Thai: หนองแหย่ง) is a *tambon* (subdistrict) of San Sai District, in Chiang Mai Province, Thailand. In 2005 it had a total population of 5,117 people. The *tambon* contains 11 villages. Source (edited): "http://en.wikipedia.org/wiki/Nong_Yaeng"

Omkoi

Omkoi (Thai: อมก๋อย) is a *tambon* (subdistrict) of Omkoi District, in Chiang Mai Province, Thailand. In 2005 it had a total population of 17,208 people. The *tambon* contains 20 villages. Source (edited): "http://en.wikipedia.org/wiki/Omkoi"

On Klang

On Klang (Thai: ออนกลาง) is a *tambon* (subdistrict) of Mae On District, in Chiang Mai Province, Thailand. In 2005 it had a total population of 4,985 people. The *tambon* contains 11 villages. Source (edited): "http://en.wikipedia.org/wiki/On_Klang"

On Nuea

On Nuea (Thai: ออนเหนือ) is a *tambon* (subdistrict) of Mae On District, in Chiang Mai Province, Thailand. In 2005 it had a total population of 3,552 people. The *tambon* contains 10 villages. Source (edited): "http://en.wikipedia.org/wiki/On_Nuea"

On Tai

On Tai (Thai: ออนใต้) is a *tambon* (subdistrict) of San Kamphaeng District, in Chiang Mai Province, Thailand. In 2005 it had a total population of 5,371 people. The *tambon* contains 11 villages. Source (edited): "http://en.wikipedia.org/wiki/On_Tai"

Pa Bong

Pa Bong (Thai: ป่าบง) is a *tambon* (subdistrict) of Saraphi District, in Chiang Mai Province, Thailand. In 2005 it had a total population of 3,506 people. The *tambon* contains 6 villages. Source (edited): "http://en.wikipedia.org/wiki/Pa_Bong"

Pa Daet, Mueang Chiang Mai

Pa Daet (Thai: ป่าแดด) is a *tambon* (subdistrict) of Mueang Chiang Mai District, in Chiang Mai Province, Thailand. In 2009 it had a total population of 16859 people.

The subdistrict is located south of the city of Chiang Mai, along the western short of the Ping River. The Muang Chiang Mai Wetland is located along this river bank within the tambon territory.

Administration

The *tambon* is subdivided into 13 administrative villages (Muban).
A small of the subdistrict is part of the city Chiang Mai, most of the area belongs to the subdistrict municipality (thesaban tambon) Pa Daet.

History

The part of the subdistrict not belonging to the city Chiang Mai became administrated by a Tambon administrative organization (TAO) in 1995. In 2007 it was upgraded to a subdistrict municipality. Source (edited): "http://en.wikipedia.org/wiki/Pa_Daet,_Mueang_Chiang_Mai"

Pa Lan

Pa Lan (Thai: ป่าลาน) is a *tambon* (subdistrict) of Doi Saket District, in Chiang Mai Province, Thailand. In 2005 it had a total population of 1,993 people. The *tambon* contains 6 villages.
Source (edited): "http://en.wikipedia.org/wiki/Pa_Lan"

Pa Miang

Pa Miang (Thai: ป่าเมี่ยง) is a *tambon* (subdistrict) of Doi Saket District, in Chiang Mai Province, Thailand. In 2005 it had a total population of 3,638 people. The *tambon* contains 6 villages.
Source (edited): "http://en.wikipedia.org/wiki/Pa_Miang"

Pa Nai

Pa Nai (Thai: ป่าไหน่) is a *tambon* (subdistrict) of Phrao District, in Chiang Mai Province, Thailand. In 2005 it had a total population of 4,799 people. The *tambon* contains 10 villages.
Source (edited): "http://en.wikipedia.org/wiki/Pa_Nai"

Pa Pae

Pa Pae may refer to:
- Pa Pae, Mae Sariang
- Pa Pae, Mae Taeng

Source (edited): "http://en.wikipedia.org/wiki/Pa_Pae"

Pa Phai

Pa Phai (Thai: ป่าไผ่) is a *tambon* (subdistrict) of San Sai District, in Chiang Mai Province, Thailand. In 2005 it had a total population of 12,459 people. The *tambon* contains 16 villages.
Source (edited): "http://en.wikipedia.org/wiki/Pa_Phai"

Pa Pong, Doi Saket

Pa Pong (Thai: ป่าป้อง) is a *tambon* (subdistrict) of Doi Saket District, in Chiang Mai Province, Thailand. In 2005 it had a total population of 3,549 people. The *tambon* contains 7 villages.
Source (edited): "http://en.wikipedia.org/wiki/Pa_Pong,_Doi_Saket"

Pa Tan, Chiang Mai

Pa Tan (Thai: ?) is a *tambon* (subdistrict) of Mueang Chiang Mai District, in Chiang Mai Province, Thailand. In 2005 it had a total population of 8,855 people.

Source (edited): "http://en.wikipedia.org/wiki/Pa_Tan,_Chiang_Mai"

Pa Tum

Pa Tum (Thai: ป่าตุ้ม) is a *tambon* (subdistrict) of Phrao District, in Chiang Mai Province, Thailand. In 2005 it had a total population of 5,475 people. The *tambon* contains 12 villages.

Source (edited): "http://en.wikipedia.org/wiki/Pa_Tum"

Pang Hin Fon

Pang Hin Fon (Thai: ปางหินฝน) is a *tambon* (subdistrict) of Mae Chaem District, in Chiang Mai Province, Thailand. In 2005 it had a total population of 6,856 people. The *tambon* contains 14 villages.

Source (edited): "http://en.wikipedia.org/wiki/Pang_Hin_Fon"

Phra Sing

Phra Sing (Thai: พระสิงห์) is a *tambon* (subdistrict) of Mueang Chiang Mai District, in Chiang Mai Province, Thailand. In 2005 it had a total population of 8,616 people.

Source (edited): "http://en.wikipedia.org/wiki/Phra_Sing"

Piang Luang

Piang Luang (Thai: เปียงหลวง) is a *tambon* (subdistrict) of Wiang Haeng District, in Chiang Mai Province, Thailand. In 2005 it had a total population of 16,757 people. The *tambon* contains 9 villages. The town lies near the border with Shan State, Burma.

Source (edited): "http://en.wikipedia.org/wiki/Piang_Luang"

Ping Khong

Ping Khong (Thai: เชียงของปิงโค้ง) is a *tambon* (subdistrict) of Chiang Dao District, in Chiang Mai Province, Thailand. In 2005 it had a total population of 11,606 people. The *tambon* contains 16 villages.

Source (edited): "http://en.wikipedia.org/wiki/Ping_Khong"

Pong Nam Ron, Fang

Pong Nam Ron (Thai: โป่งน้ำร้อน) is a *tambon* (subdistrict) of Fang District, in Chiang Mai Province, Thailand. In 2009 it had a total population of 5687 people. The *tambon* contains 7 villages.

Source (edited): "http://en.wikipedia.org/wiki/Pong_Nam_Ron,_Fang"

Pong Tam

Pong Tam (Thai: ปงตำ) is a *tambon* (subdistrict) of Chai Prakan District, in Chiang Mai Province, Thailand. In 2005 it had a total population of 8,267 people. The *tambon* contains 8 villages.

Source (edited): "http://en.wikipedia.org/wiki/Pong_Tam"

Pong Thung

Pong Thung (Thai: โป่งทุ่ง) is a *tambon* (subdistrict) of Doi Tao District, in Chiang Mai Province, Thailand. In 2005 it had a total population of 6,407 people. The *tambon* contains 11 villages. Source (edited): "http://en.wikipedia.org/wiki/Pong_Thung"

Pong Yaeng

Pong Yaeng (Thai: โป่งแยง) is a *tambon* (subdistrict) of Mae Rim District, in Chiang Mai Province, Thailand. In 2005 it had a total population of 9,922 people. The *tambon* contains 9 villages. Source (edited): "http://en.wikipedia.org/wiki/Pong_Yaeng"

Rim Nuea

Rim Nuea (Thai: ริมเหนือ) is a *tambon* (subdistrict) of Mae Rim District, in Chiang Mai Province, Thailand. In 2005 it had a total population of 3,336 people. The *tambon* contains 4 villages. Source (edited): "http://en.wikipedia.org/wiki/Rim_Nuea"

Rim Tai

Rim Tai (Thai: ริมใต้) is a *tambon* (subdistrict) of Mae Rim District, in Chiang Mai Province, Thailand. In 2005 it had a total population of 9,498 people. The *tambon* contains 8 villages. Source (edited): "http://en.wikipedia.org/wiki/Rim_Tai"

Rong Wua Daeng

Rong Wua Daeng (Thai: ร้องวัวแดง) is a *tambon* (subdistrict) of San Kamphaeng District, in Chiang Mai Province, Thailand. In 2005 it had a total population of 5,718 people. The *tambon* contains 11 villages. Source (edited): "http://en.wikipedia.org/wiki/Rong_Wua_Daeng"

Sa-nga Ban

Sa-nga Ban (Thai: สง่าบ้าน) is a *tambon* (subdistrict) of Doi Saket District, in Chiang Mai Province, Thailand. In 2005 it had a total population of 2,225 people. The *tambon* contains 5 villages. Source (edited): "http://en.wikipedia.org/wiki/Sa-nga_Ban"

Saen Hai

Saen Hai (Thai: แสนไห) is a *tambon* (subdistrict) of Wiang Haeng District, in Chiang Mai Province, Thailand. In 2005 it had a total population of 3,488 people. The *tambon* contains 5 villages. Source (edited): "http://en.wikipedia.org/wiki/Saen_Hai"

Sai Mun, San Kamphaeng

Sai Mun (Thai: ทรายมูล) is a *tambon* (subdistrict) of San Kamphaeng District, in Chiang Mai Province, Thailand. In 2005 it had a total population of 4,230 people. The *tambon* contains 7 villages. Source (edited): "http://en.wikipedia.org/wiki/Sai_Mun,_San_Kamphaeng"

Saluang, Mae Rim

Saluang (Thai: สะลวง) is a *tambon* (subdistrict) of Mae Rim District, in Chiang Mai Province, Thailand. In 2005 it had a total population of 4731 people. The *tambon* contains 8 villages. Source (edited): "http://en.wikipedia.org/wiki/Saluang,_Mae_Rim"

Samoeng Nuea

Samoeng Nuea (Thai: สะเมิงเหนือ) is a *tambon* (subdistrict) of Samoeng District, in Chiang Mai Province, Thailand. In 2005 it had a total population of 3,426 people. The *tambon* contains 6 villages. Source (edited): "http://en.wikipedia.org/wiki/Samoeng_Nuea"

Samoeng Tai

Samoeng Tai (Thai: สะเมิงใต้) is a *tambon* (subdistrict) of Samoeng District, in Chiang Mai Province, Thailand. In 2005 it had a total population of 5,366 people. The *tambon* contains 11 villages. Source (edited): "http://en.wikipedia.org/wiki/Samoeng_Tai"

Samran Rat

Samran Rat (Thai: สำราญราษฎร์) is a *tambon* (subdistrict) of Doi Saket District, in Chiang Mai Province, Thailand. In 2005 it had a total population of 3,336 people. The *tambon* contains 8 villages. Source (edited): "http://en.wikipedia.org/wiki/Samran_Rat"

San Kamphaeng

San Kamphaeng (Thai: สันกำแพง) is a town and *tambon* (subdistrict) of San Kamphaeng District, in Chiang Mai Province, Thailand. In 2005 it had a total population of 13,686 people. The *tambon* contains 14 villages. Source (edited): "http://en.wikipedia.org/wiki/San_Kamphaeng"

San Klang, San Kamphaeng

San Klang (Thai: สันกลาง) is a *tambon* (subdistrict) of San Kamphaeng District, in Chiang Mai Province, Thailand. In 2005 it had a total population of 6,088 people. The *tambon* contains 8 villages. Source (edited): "http://en.wikipedia.org/wiki/San_Klang,_San_Kamphaeng"

San Klang, San Pa Tong

San Klang (Thai: สันกลาง) is a *tambon* (subdistrict) of San Pa Tong District, in Chiang Mai Province, Thailand. In 2005 it had a total population of 4,478 people. The *tambon* contains 9 villages. Source (edited): "http://en.wikipedia.org/wiki/San_Klang,_San_Pa_Tong"

San Maha Phon

San Maha Phon (Thai: สันมหาพน) is a *tambon* (subdistrict) of Mae Taeng District, in Chiang Mai Province, Thailand. In 2005 it had a total population of 6,660 people. The *tambon* contains 10 villages. Source (edited): "http://en.wikipedia.org/wiki/San_Maha_Phon"

San Na Meng

San Na Meng (Thai: สันนาเม็ง) is a *tambon* (subdistrict) of San Sai District, in Chiang Mai Province, Thailand.In 2005 it had a total population of 8,100 people. The *tambon* contains 10 villages. Source (edited): "http://en.wikipedia.org/wiki/San_Na_Meng"

San Pa Pao

San Pa Pao (Thai: สันป่าเปา) is a *tambon* (subdistrict) of San Sai District, in Chiang Mai Province, Thailand.In 2005 it had a total population of 3,934 people. The *tambon* contains 6 villages. Source (edited): "http://en.wikipedia.org/wiki/San_Pa_Pao"

San Pa Yang

San Pa Yang (Thai: สันป่ายาง) is a *tambon* (subdistrict) of Mae Taeng District, in Chiang Mai Province, Thailand.In 2005 it had a total population of 4,637 people. The *tambon* contains 5 villages. Source (edited): "http://en.wikipedia.org/wiki/San_Pa_Yang"

San Phak Wan

San Phak Wan (Thai: สันผักหวาน) is a *tambon* (subdistrict) of Hang Dong District, in Chiang Mai Province, Thailand.In 2005 it had a total population of 8928 people. The *tambon* contains 7 villages. Source (edited): "http://en.wikipedia.org/wiki/San_Phak_Wan"

San Phi Suea

San Phi Suea (Thai: สันผีเสื้อ) is a *tambon* (subdistrict) of Mueang Chiang Mai District, in Chiang Mai Province, Thailand.In 2005 it had a total population of 8,466 people. The *tambon* contains 9 villages. Source (edited): "http://en.wikipedia.org/wiki/San_Phi_Suea"

San Phranet

San Phranet (Thai: สันพระเนตร) is a *tambon* (subdistrict) of San Sai District, in Chiang Mai Province, Thailand.In 2005 it had a total population of 5,965 people. The *tambon* contains 7 villages. Source (edited): "http://en.wikipedia.org/wiki/San_Phranet"

San Pong

San Pong (Thai: สันโป่ง) is a *tambon* (subdistrict) of Mae Rim District, in Chiang Mai Province, Thailand.In 2005 it had a total population of 9,425 people. The *tambon* contains 11 villages. Source (edited): "http://en.wikipedia.org/wiki/San_Pong"

San Pu Loei

San Pu Loei (Thai: สันปูเลย) is a *tambon* (subdistrict) of Doi Saket District, in Chiang Mai Province, Thailand.In 2005 it had a total population of 9,137 people. The *tambon* contains 14 villages. Source (edited): "http://en.wikipedia.org/wiki/San_Pu_Loei"

San Sai, Fang

San Sai (Thai: สันทราย) is a *tambon* (subdistrict) of Fang District, in Chiang Mai Province, Thailand.In 2005 it had a total population of 11,583 people. The *tambon* contains 17 villages. Source (edited): "http://en.wikipedia.org/wiki/San_Sai,_Fang"

San Sai, Phrao

San Sai (Thai: สันทราย) is a *tambon* (subdistrict) of Phrao District, in Chiang Mai Province, Thailand.In 2005 it had a total population of 6,646 people. The *tambon* contains 15 villages. Source (edited): "http://en.wikipedia.org/wiki/San_Sai,_Phrao"

San Sai, Saraphi

San Sai (Thai: สันทราย) is a *tambon* (subdistrict) of Saraphi District, in Chiang Mai Province, Thailand.In 2005 it had a total population of 5,635 people. The *tambon* contains 12 villages. Source (edited): "http://en.wikipedia.org/wiki/San_Sai,_Saraphi"

San Sai Luang

San Sai Luang (Thai: สันทรายหลวง) is a *tambon* (subdistrict) of San Sai District, in Chiang Mai Province, Thailand.In 2005 it had a total population of 6,397 people. The *tambon* contains 8 villages. Source (edited): "http://en.wikipedia.org/wiki/San_Sai_Luang"

San Sai Noi

San Sai Noi (Thai: สันทรายน้อย) is a *tambon* (subdistrict) of San Sai District, in Chiang Mai Province, Thailand.In 2005 it had a total population of 13,950 people. The *tambon* contains 7 villages. Source (edited): "http://en.wikipedia.org/wiki/San_Sai_Noi"

San Ton Mue

San Ton Mue (Thai: สันต้นหมื้อ) is a *tambon* (subdistrict) of Mae Ai District, in Chiang Mai Province, Thailand.In 2005 it had a total population of 6,668 people. The *tambon* contains 13 villages. Source (edited): "http://en.wikipedia.org/wiki/San_Ton_Mue"

Santi Suk

Santi Suk may refer to:
- Santi Suk, Chiang Mai
- Santi Suk, Chiang Rai

Source (edited): "http://en.wikipedia.org/wiki/Santi_Suk"

Saraphi

Saraphi (Thai: สารภีสารภี) is a *tambon* (subdistrict) of Saraphi District, in Chiang Mai Province, Thailand.In 2005 it had a total population of 6,959 people. The *tambon* contains 9 villages. Source (edited): "http://en.wikipedia.org/wiki/Saraphi"

Si Dong Yen

Si Dong Yen (Thai: ศรีดงเย็น) is a *tambon* (subdistrict) of Chai Prakan District, in Chiang Mai Province, Thailand.In 2005 it had a total population of 15,842 people. The *tambon* contains 18 villages.
Source (edited): "http://en.wikipedia.org/wiki/Si_Dong_Yen"

Si Phum

Si Phum (Thai: ?) is a *tambon* (subdistrict) of Mueang Chiang Mai District, in Chiang Mai Province, Thailand.In 2005 it had a total population of 17,610 people.
Source (edited): "http://en.wikipedia.org/wiki/Si_Phum"

Song Khwae

Song Khwae may refer to:
- Song Khwae (district), a district (Amphoe) in the northwestern part of Nan Province, northern Thailand.
- Song Khwae (tambon), a subdistrict (tambon) of Doi Lo District, in Chiang Mai Province, Thailand.

Source (edited): "http://en.wikipedia.org/wiki/Song_Khwae"

Sop Khong

Sop Khong (Thai: สบโขง) is a small town and *tambon* (subdistrict) of Omkoi District, in Chiang Mai Province, Thailand.In 2005 it had a total population of 6,285 people. The *tambon* contains 12 villages. It lies within the Mae Ngao National Park.
Source (edited): "http://en.wikipedia.org/wiki/Sop_Khong"

Sop Mae Kha

Sop Mae Kha (Thai: สบแม่ข่า) is a *tambon* (subdistrict) of Hang Dong District, in Chiang Mai Province, Thailand.In 2005 it had a total population of 2405 people. The *tambon* contains 5 villages.
Source (edited): "http://en.wikipedia.org/wiki/Sop_Mae_Kha"

Sop Poeng

Sop Poeng (Thai: สบเปิง) is a *tambon* (subdistrict) of Mae Taeng District, in Chiang Mai Province, Thailand.In 2005 it had a total population of 7,977 people. The *tambon* contains 13 villages.
Source (edited): "http://en.wikipedia.org/wiki/Sop_Poeng"

Sop Tia

Sop Tia (Thai: สบเตี๊ยะ) is a *tambon* (subdistrict) of Chom Thong District, in Chiang Mai Province, Thailand.In 2005 it had a total population of 12,739 people. The *tambon* contains 20 villages.
Source (edited): "http://en.wikipedia.org/wiki/Sop_Tia"

Suthep

Suthep (Thai: สุเทพ) is a *tambon* (subdistrict) of Mueang Chiang Mai District, in Chiang Mai Province, Thailand.In 2005 it had a total population of 36,952 people. The *tambon* contains 15 villages.
Source (edited): "http://en.wikipedia.org/wiki/Suthep"

Talat Khwan

Talat Khwan (Thai: ตลาดขวัญ) is a *tambon* (subdistrict) of Doi Saket District, in Chiang Mai Province, Thailand. In 2005 it had a total population of 3,418 people. The *tambon* contains 6 villages.

Source (edited): "http://en.wikipedia.org/wiki/Talat_Khwan"

Talat Yai

Talat Yai (Thai: ตลาดใหญ่) is a *tambon* (subdistrict) of Doi Saket District, in Chiang Mai Province, Thailand. In 2005 it had a total population of 3,760 people. The *tambon* contains 5 villages.

Source (edited): "http://en.wikipedia.org/wiki/Talat_Yai"

Tha Duea

Tha Duea (Thai: ท่าเดื่อ) is a *tambon* (subdistrict) of Doi Tao District, in Chiang Mai Province, Thailand. In 2005 it had a total population of 3242 people. The *tambon* contains 6 villages.

Source (edited): "http://en.wikipedia.org/wiki/Tha_Duea"

Tha Kwang

Tha Kwang (Thai: ท่ากว้าง) is a *tambon* (subdistrict) of Saraphi District, in Chiang Mai Province, Thailand. In 2005 it had a total population of 2,856 people. The *tambon* contains 7 villages.

Source (edited): "http://en.wikipedia.org/wiki/Tha_Kwang"

Tha Nuea

Tha Nuea (Thai: ทาเหนือ) is a *tambon* (subdistrict) of Mae On District, in Chiang Mai Province, Thailand. In 2005 it had a total population of 2,372 people. The *tambon* contains 5 villages.

Source (edited): "http://en.wikipedia.org/wiki/Tha_Nuea"

Tha Pha, Mae Chaem

Tha Pha (Thai: ท่าผา) is a *tambon* (subdistrict) of Mae Chaem District, in Chiang Mai Province, Thailand. In 2005 it had a total population of 4,952 people. The *tambon* contains 14 villages.

Source (edited): "http://en.wikipedia.org/wiki/Tha_Pha,_Mae_Chaem"

Tha Sala, Mueang Chiang Mai

Tha Sala (Thai: ท่าศาลา) is a *tambon* (subdistrict) of Mueang Chiang Mai District, in Chiang Mai Province, Thailand. In 2005 it had a total population of 11,347 people. The *tambon* contains 5 villages.

Source (edited): "http://en.wikipedia.org/wiki/Tha_Sala,_Mueang_Chiang_Mai"

Tha Ton

Tha Ton (Thai: ท่าตอน) is a subdistrict (*tambon*) of Mae Ai district in the far north of Chiang Mai Province in Thailand. The town is situated on the Kok River near the border with Myanmar, about a 3-hour drive north of the city of Chiang Mai. The central village of the subdistrict is **Ban Tha Ton**.

History

The river forms part of the border and consequently the village has changed hands numerous times in the turbulent history of the area with the latest change happening in the early 20th century when the border was moved two miles upstream leaving the north bank, previously part of Burma (Myanmar), to

Thailand. This part of Thaton, known in Thai as Ban Rom Thai, is inhabited by the Shan ethnic group. The area around Thaton is populated by various hill tribes including Yao, Lisu, Lahu, Karen and Akha. Thaton is also home to Chinese nationalists forced to further flee from their home-in-exile after the coup in Burma.

Administration
The subdistrict is administrated by a Tambon administrative organization (TAO). It is subdivided into 19 villages (*muban*).

Tourism
Thaton is located on the widely travelled tourist route between Chiang Mai and Chiang Rai. Since the 1970s, riverboat trips between Chiang Rai and Thaton have given foreign tourist as well as native Thais the opportunity to visit remote jungles, observe different ethnic groups, and see the Fang Plain, bringing a welcome influx of capital into the local economy. In the 1980s, this trend continued with the building of several small resorts to accommodate tourists.

Wat Thaton
The village is overlooked by a striking hilltop Buddhist temple known as Wat Tha Ton. The temple complex includes four huge statues of the Buddha, two in typical Thai style and two showing Chinese influence. One of these, the Standing Buddha, is over 35 feet tall.
Source (edited): "http://en.wikipedia.org/wiki/Tha_Ton"

Tha Wang Phrao

Tha Wang Phrao (Thai: ท่าวังพร้าว) is a *tambon* (subdistrict) of San Pa Tong District, in Chiang Mai Province, Thailand.In 2005 it had a total population of 3697 people. The *tambon* contains 7 villages.
Source (edited): "http://en.wikipedia.org/wiki/Tha_Wang_Phrao"

Tha Wang Tan

Tha Wang Tan (Thai: ท่าวังตาล) is a *tambon* (subdistrict) of Saraphi District, in Chiang Mai Province, Thailand.In 2005 it had a total population of 9,299 people. The *tambon* contains 13 villages.
Source (edited): "http://en.wikipedia.org/wiki/Tha_Wang_Tan"

Thep Sadet

Thep Sadet (Thai: เทพเสด็จ) is a *tambon* (subdistrict) of Doi Saket District, in Chiang Mai Province, Thailand.In 2005 it had a total population of 1,716 people. The *tambon* contains 8 villages.
Source (edited): "http://en.wikipedia.org/wiki/Thep_Sadet"

Thung Khao Phuang

Thung Khao Phuang (Thai: ทุ่งข้าวพวง) is a *tambon* (subdistrict) of Chiang Dao District, in Chiang Mai Province, Thailand.In 2005 it had a total population of 9,009 people. The *tambon* contains 7 villages.
Source (edited): "http://en.wikipedia.org/wiki/Thung_Khao_Phuang"

Thung Luang, Phrao

Thung Luang (Thai: ทุ่งหลวง) is a *tambon* (subdistrict) of Phrao District, in Chiang Mai Province, Thailand.In 2005 it had a total population of 1,821 people. The *tambon* contains 6 villages.
Source (edited): "http://en.wikipedia.org/wiki/Thung_Luang,_Phrao"

Thung Pi

Thung Pi (Thai: ทุ่งปี๊) is a *tambon* (subdistrict) of Mae Wang District, in Chiang Mai Province, Thailand.In 2005 it had a total population of 4,602 people. The *tambon* contains 12 villages.
Source (edited): "http://en.wikipedia.org/wiki/Thung_Pi"

Thung Ruang Thong, Mae Wang

Thung Ruang Thong (Thai: ทุ่งรวงทอง) is a *tambon* (subdistrict) of Mae Wang District, in Chiang Mai Province, Thailand.In 2005 it had a total population of 2,650 people. The *tambon* contains 8 villages.

Source (edited): "http://en.wikipedia.org/wiki/Thung_Ruang_Thong,_Mae_Wang"

Thung Satok

Thung Satok (Thai: ทุ่งสะโตก) is a *tambon* (subdistrict) of San Pa Tong District, in Chiang Mai Province, Thailand.In 2005 it had a total population of 6,707 people. The *tambon* contains 12 villages.

Source (edited): "http://en.wikipedia.org/wiki/Thung_Satok"

Thung Tom

Thung Tom (Thai: ทุ่งต้อม) is a *tambon* (subdistrict) of San Pa Tong District, in Chiang Mai Province, Thailand.In 2005 it had a total population of 7,405 people. The *tambon* contains 11 villages.

Source (edited): "http://en.wikipedia.org/wiki/Thung_Tom"

Ton Pao

Ton Pao (Thai: ต้นเปา) is a *tambon* (subdistrict) of San Kamphaeng District, in Chiang Mai Province, Thailand.In 2005 it had a total population of 11,006 people. The *tambon* contains 10 villages.

Source (edited): "http://en.wikipedia.org/wiki/Ton_Pao"

Wat Ket

Wat Ket (Thai: วัดเกต) is a *tambon* (subdistrict) of Mueang Chiang Mai District, in Chiang Mai Province, Thailand.In 2005 it had a total population of 24,094 people.

Source (edited): "http://en.wikipedia.org/wiki/Wat_Ket"

Wiang, Fang

Wiang (Thai: เวียง) is a *tambon* (subdistrict) of Fang District, in Chiang Mai Province, Thailand.In 2005 it had a total population of 26,810 people. The *tambon* contains 19 villages.

Source (edited): "http://en.wikipedia.org/wiki/Wiang,_Fang"

Wiang, Phrao

Wiang (Thai: ?) is a *tambon* (subdistrict) of Phrao District, in Chiang Mai Province, Thailand.In 2005 it had a total population of 3,803 people. The *tambon* contains 6 villages.

Source (edited): "http://en.wikipedia.org/wiki/Wiang,_Phrao"

Yang Khram

Yang Khram (Thai: ยางคราม) is a *tambon* (subdistrict) of Doi Lo District, in Chiang Mai Province, Thailand.In 2005 it had a total population of 5182 people. The *tambon* contains 11 villages.

Source (edited): "http://en.wikipedia.org/wiki/Yang_Khram"

Yang Moen

Yang Moen (Thai: ยั้งเมิน) is a *tambon* (subdistrict) of Samoeng District, in Chiang Mai Province, Thailand.In 2005 it had a total population of 3,845 people. The *tambon* contains 8 villages. Source (edited): "http://en.wikipedia.org/wiki/Yang_Moen"

Yang Noeng

Yang Noeng (Thai: ยางเนิ้ง) is a *tambon* (subdistrict) of Saraphi District, in Chiang Mai Province, Thailand.In 2005 it had a total population of 8,964 people. The *tambon* contains 7 villages. Source (edited): "http://en.wikipedia.org/wiki/Yang_Noeng"

Yang Piang

Yang Piang (Thai: ยางเปียง) is a *tambon* (subdistrict) of Omkoi District, in Chiang Mai Province, Thailand.In 2005 it had a total population of 7,990 people. The *tambon* contains 17 villages. Source (edited): "http://en.wikipedia.org/wiki/Yang_Piang"

Yu Wa

Yu Wa (Thai: ยุหว่า) is a *tambon* (subdistrict) of San Pa Tong District, in Chiang Mai Province, Thailand.In 2005 it had a total population of 13,175 people. The *tambon* contains 14 villages. Source (edited): "http://en.wikipedia.org/wiki/Yu_Wa"